A Heart
that
Hopes
in God

CATHERINE MARTIN

A HEART THAT HOPES IN GOD

QuietTime
MINISTRIES
PALM DESERT, CALIFORNIA

A Heart That Hopes In God—Truths From The Psalms To Anchor Your Soul
Copyright © 2007 by Catherine Martin
Published by Quiet Time Ministries
Palm Desert, California 92255
www.quiettime.org

ISBN-13: 978-0-9766886-5-5

Second Edition published by Quiet Time Ministries 2011

Printed in the United States of America
11 12 13 14 15 16 17 18 19 / LSI / 11 10 9 8 7 6 5 4 3 2

Dedicated to…
the One who is my living Hope,
the Lord Jesus Christ.

Dedicated to my husband
David Martin,
who has been my dear companion
for twenty-nine years
on this journey of hope.

Dedicated to
all those hearts that have hoped in God
in every generation.
Thank you for being my example
of how to run my race by faith
and hope in the promises of God.
Thank you for your faithfulness to
find the promise
embrace the promise
trust the promise
live the promise.

May our names be added
to the list of those who have…
a heart that hopes in God.

For whatever was written in earlier times
was written for our instruction,
so that through perseverance
and the encouragement of the Scriptures
we might have hope.

ROMANS 15:4

⁓⁓

This hope we have as an anchor of the soul,
a hope both sure and steadfast
and one which enters within the veil…

HEBREWS 6:19

⁓⁓

Now may the God of hope
fill you with all joy and peace in believing,
so that you will abound in hope
by the power of the Holy Spirit.

ROMANS 15:13

CONTENTS

INTRODUCTION

Horatio Spafford planned a vacation for his family in England to hear the preaching of D.L. Moody. He sent his wife and four daughters ahead on the S.S. Ville du Havre. He would join them in a few days. Their ship was struck by another vessel and sank in twelve minutes. Over two hundred people died that day including Spafford's daughters. He received the following cable from his wife, "Saved alone." He boarded the next ship to be with his wife. During his journey across the Atlantic, the captain pointed to the place where the Ville du Havre sank.

What does a person do when the very worst imaginable thing happens, life is altered, and there is seemingly no hope to change things? In the midst of his great loss, Horatio Spafford sat down and wrote the beloved hymn that has comforted countless hearts, It Is Well With My Soul. The words go like this: "When peace like a river attendeth my way, when sorrows like sea-billows roll; whatever my lot, Thou hast taught me to say, It is well, it is well with my soul. As the hymn continues, one can see what brought peace to Horatio Spafford's soul: My sin—O, the bliss of this glorious thought, My sin—not in part but the whole, is nailed to the cross and I bear it no more, Praise the Lord, praise the Lord, O my soul." It was a truth from God's Word, a promise of forgiveness because of the death of Christ that gave Spafford hope. This truth, this promise was a certainty that held his soul in place in the midst of dramatic, life-altering change. Focusing on God's truth led him to the greatest promise of all: "And Lord, haste the day when my faith shall be sight, the clouds be rolled back as a scroll, the trump shall resound and the Lord shall descend, praise the Lord, praise the Lord, O my soul." Finally his eyes were lifted beyond the here and now of this temporal life to an eternal future with the Lord—and that brought ultimate comfort to his soul. One day soon he would be face to face with His Lord and reunited with his daughters.

I have always been drawn to stories of hope in the midst of suffering. To me that is where the rubber meets the road in life. It is one thing to sing while the sun is shining but quite another when the thick dark clouds roll in. I remember years ago reading *Evidence Unseen*, the story of the imprisonment of Darlene Deibler Rose during World War II and the loss of her husband. I sobbed uncontrollably through every page of that book. Her suffering was so devastating to me. And yet she stood strong in her faith in God. Corrie ten Boom held on to the Lord during her time at Ravensbruck concentration camp. John Bunyan wrote *Pilgrim's Progress* while imprisoned. Hannah Whitall Smith, while in a difficult marriage, wrote *The Christian's Secret Of A Happy Life*. How did they make it? How could they have such hope? There is a secret I've discovered in their lives and in my own life as well. They laid hold of the truth of God's Word, His promises found in the Bible. The result—it was well with their soul.

When I read the story of Darlene Rose I had no idea of the devastating losses and suffering ahead for me in my own life over the years. I remember one trial in particular early on in my relationship with the Lord. The fire of that time of suffering was so fierce that I wanted to get in my car and drive off into the sunset. There was one thing that kept me from doing it—the truths I found in the Word of God. I read 1 Peter 4:12, "Beloved, do not be surprised at the fiery ordeal among you, which comes upon you for your testing, as though some strange thing were happening to you; but to the degree that you share the sufferings of Christ, keep on rejoicing, so that also at the revelation of His glory you may rejoice with exultation." I learned what to do in 1 Peter 4:19, "Therefore, those also who suffer according to the will of God shall entrust their souls to a faithful Creator in doing what is right." Now I have discovered that the most difficult action in the midst of a devastating change or loss in life is to entrust my soul to the Lord. There is one place I always run when I am hurting because of a trial or suffering in my own life: the Psalms. The promises from my Lord in the Psalms enable me to run to the arms of God and entrust my soul to Him. And then, it is well with my soul. My circumstance may not change, but my heart is near to God, and peace floods my soul. God's Word anchors my soul and I have hope.

There is so much to discover in the Psalms. They are filled with truth about God: who He is and what He does. In the Psalms you learn how to sing in the darkness of the night. The Psalms are the healing balm for the soul bringing comfort to a wounded heart. I know because I have experienced the blessed benefit of the Psalms through all my darkest days and nights. And so have many others. Spurgeon said, "The delightful study of the Psalms has yielded me boundless profit and ever-growing pleasure." I echo his gratitude for the gift of the Psalms. I love the Psalms so much that I've collected many commentaries on them where I can linger, explore, and mine them for the great treasure they hold.

A Heart That Hopes In God is going to take you deep into some of the choice Psalms of comfort to bring you hope. You need God's kind of hope no matter what circumstances you are experiencing in life. Hope is the fuel that lights the fire of your heart to make you burn with love for the Lord and continue on in the great adventure of knowing God. You see, biblical hope is different than the kind of hope found in the world. Worldly hope is a wishing or wanting that is fixed on something that may or may not happen. But God's kind of hope is a certainty based on fact; it looks at the promises found in the Bible, His Word. You will find that the truth sets you free— free to soar in life even when faced with obstacles and adversities.

Together we will embark on this journey through Scripture in the form of quiet times alone with the Lord. Each quiet time is organized according to the PRAYER™ Quiet Time Plan™:

Prepare Your Heart

Read and Study God's Word

Adore God in Prayer

Yield Yourself to God

Enjoy His Presence

Rest in His Love

Each week consists of five days of quiet times and then a devotional reading on Days 6-7. Each quiet time includes devotional reading, devotional Bible study, journaling, prayer, worship, hymns, and application of God's Word. Journal Pages and Prayer Pages (adapted from The Quiet Time Notebook™) to record your thoughts and prayers are in the back of this book. With *A Heart That Hopes In God* and your Bible you have everything you need for quiet time with the Lord. Because schedules vary, you can be flexible and may choose to take more than one day for each quiet time. You may complete each quiet time at your own pace, taking as little or as much time as you can give to spend alone with the Lord. If you desire to learn more about how to have a quiet time, I encourage you to get my book *Six Secrets to a Powerful Quiet Time*. To learn more about different kinds of devotional Bible studies for your quiet time, I encourage you to read my book *Knowing and Loving the Bible*.

VIEWER GUIDES

At the end of each week you will find your Viewer Guide to take notes from the video message. In each message, Catherine teaches from God's Word, and challenges you to draw near to the Lord. These messages are especially designed to accompany your studies each week. These videos messages are available on the companion *A Heart That Hopes In God* DVDs or as Downloadable M4V Video messages. These messages are also available on Audio CDs and as Downloadable MP3 Audio messages. Search the Quiet Time Ministries Online Store at www.quiettime.org or call Quiet Time Ministries at 1-800-925-6458.

FOR LEADERS

A Heart That Hopes In God is a powerful resource for group study including a complete Leader's Guide with Discussion Questions in the Appendix. *A Heart That Hopes In God* DVD Leader's Kits are available at the Quiet Time Ministries Online Store at www.quiettime.org. You may also call Quiet Time Ministries at 1-800-925-6458. *A Heart That Hopes In God* is available as a 1-book Leader's Kit or a 10-book Leader's Kit. The kit includes the *A Heart That Hopes In God* book(s), *A Heart That Hopes In God* DVDs with 9 video messages, *A Heart That Hopes In God* Journal, and the Quiet Time Ministries Signature Tote. Each *A Heart That Hopes In God* book is organized into 8 weeks with 5 days of quiet time per week and Days 6-7 for review and meditation. The book also includes 9 Viewer Guides for the group video sessions, Leader's Guide and Discussion Questions, and Journal and Prayer Pages.

QUIET TIME MINISTRIES ONLINE

Quiet Time Ministries Online at www.quiettime.org is a place where you can deepen your devotion to God and His Word. Cath's Blog is where Catherine shares about life, about the Lord, and just about everything else. A Walk In Grace™ is Catherine's devotional photojournal, highlighting her own photography, where you can grow deep in the garden of His grace. Quiet Time Ministries proudly sponsors Ministry For Women at www.ministryforwomen.com—a social network community for women worldwide to grow in their relationship with Jesus Christ. Connect, study, and grow at Ministry For Women.

MY LETTER TO THE LORD

As you begin these quiet times, I'd like to ask, where are you? What has been happening in your life over the last year or so? What has been your life experience? What are you facing and what has God been teaching you? It is no accident that you are in this book of quiet times, *A Heart That Hopes In God*. In fact, God has something He wants you to know, something that will change the whole landscape of your experience with Him. Watch for it, listen for it, and when you learn it, write it down and never let it go. Will you write a prayer in the form of a letter to the Lord in the space provided expressing all that is on your heart and ask Him to speak to you in these quiet times?

My Letter To The Lord

Viewer Guide
INTRODUCTION WEEK

What We Need These Days

Welcome to *A Heart That Hopes In God*, a study on hope in the Psalms. In this study in God's Word, you are going to discover truths that will anchor your soul when the storms of life you're your way. These Viewer Guides are designed to give you a place to write notes from my *A Heart That Hopes In God* messages available on DVD, Audio CD, or Downloadable M4V Video and Downloadable MP3 Audio for your computer or mobile device. In our time together today, we want to look at the healing properties of God's Word and how God uses it to give us hope when we need it most.

"For whatever was written in earlier times was written for our instruction, so that through perseverance and the encouragement of the Scriptures we might have hope" (Romans 15:4).

What we see here is that the Word of God is medicine for the _____.

How does God use the medicine of the Word in our lives?

1. God will _____to you today in His Word.

The Bible is _____for you today.

The Word of God never grows _____and it never grows _____.
Hebrews 4:12, Jeremiah 15:16

You must open the Word of God and _____it.

2. The Lord will _____you in His Word.

The Bible was written for our instruction (Romans 15:4) Instruction is *didaskalia* and means *that which is taught.*

We must be _____.
Luke 10:38-42

3. The Lord will _____you in His Word.

The word for *comfort* is *paraklesis* and means *exhortation, encouragement, and comfort for the purpose of strengthening and encouraging in the faith.*

It literally means that the Word of God _____you in your heart.

The Word of God _____your perspective.

The Word of God _____you.

What will it take for your to experience the Word of God as medicine for your heart?

_____

Hupomone – the spirit which bears things not with passive resignation but with blazing hope.

Perseverance grows in your life through _____.

It means that you _____for God's Word to work in your life.

What is the result?

_____

Elpis – the desire of some good with expectation of obtaining it.

Hope is the ability to _____to the truth of God's Word.

❧   *Video messages are available on DVDs or as Downloadable M4V Video. Audio messages are available on Audio CDs or as Downloadable MP3 Audio. Visit the Quiet Time Ministries Online Store at www.quiettime.org.*

THERE IS ALWAYS HOPE NO MATTER WHAT

Romans 15:13

Other men see only a hopeless end, but the Christian rejoices in an endless hope.

GILBERT BEEKEN

THE CERTAINTY OF HOPE

Now may the God of hope fill you with all joy and peace in believing,
so that you will abound in hope by the power of the Holy Spirit.
ROMANS 15:13

PREPARE YOUR HEART

Life is a journey of the heart leading you into a rich, deep intimacy with God. In your life with God, there are two certainties you can count on: trials and God. And you need to know God always outweighs any trial that comes your way. The secret to preventing a fall into despair is to calculate God into every circumstance.

If you have lived for any length of time you have already discovered that there are times when you are faced with adversities and obstacles that are seemingly impossible. Jesus told His followers, "In the world you have tribulation, but take courage; I have overcome the world" (John 16:33). Charles Haddon Spurgeon, the prince of preachers in England, knew what it was to face the fiery trial. In spite of physical challenges and a battle with depression, he never gave up. Why? Because of the other certainty that may be relied upon by any child of God. There is a promise so great, so abundant, that no matter what you face in life, you can have hope. The promise is found in the words of Paul in Romans 15:13, "Now may the God of hope fill you with all joy and peace in believing, so that you will abound in hope by the power of the Holy Spirit." What God is promising here is that He will fill you with joy, peace, and abundant, overflowing hope through the power of the Holy Spirit living in you. God's work in you as the God of hope allows you to live a life that does not count on favorable circumstances, but instead counts on the certainty and fact and truth and reality of God and His Word.

In this first week of your quiet time experience in the Psalms you are going to learn all about hope. It is an important part of the journey because the hope given by God is very different than the kind of hope most people count on in life. As you begin your quiet time today with the Lord take a moment and talk with the Lord. Ask Him to quiet your heart and speak to you from His Word. Then, ask Him to open the eyes of your heart and teach you all about hope. As a preparation of heart, read Psalm 1:1-3. After reading from Psalm 1, write a prayer to the Lord in your journal found in the back of this book, expressing all that is on your heart today.

READ AND STUDY GOD'S WORD

1. Read the following translations of Romans 15:13 and underline those phrases or words that are significant to you.

"Now may the God of hope fill you with all joy and peace in believing, so that you will abound in hope by the power of the Holy Spirit."
Romans 15:13 NASB

"So I pray that God, who gives you hope, will keep you happy and full of peace as you believe in him. May you overflow with hope through the power of the Holy Spirit."
Romans 15:13 NLT

"May the God of hope fill you with joy and peace in your faith, that by the power of the Holy Spirit, your whole life and outlook may be radiant with hope."
Romans 15:13 PHILLIPS

"I pray that the God who gives hope will fill you with much joy and peace while you trust in Him. Then your hope will overflow by the power of the Holy Spirit."
Romans 15:13 NCV

2. As you look at these verses do you notice what God does, what kind of hope He wants you to have, and the quality of life He intends for you? As you think about these things, what is significant to you today? What truth can you take with you and think about throughout the day?

ADORE GOD IN PRAYER

Use the words of this prayer by Spurgeon, personalizing them to fit your own circumstance:

"Oh God, Thou knowest the burden of every heart before Thee, the secret sighing of the prisoner cometh up into Thine ears. Some of us are in perplexity, others are in actual suffering of body. Some are sorely cast down in themselves, and others deeply afflicted with the trials of those they love, but as for all these burdens our soul would cast them on the Lord. In quietness and confidence shall be our strength, and we take up the place of sitting still, leaving with quiet acquiescence everything in the hands of God. Great Helmsman, Thou shalt steer the ship and we will not be troubled. By Thy grace we will leave everything most sweetly in Thy hands. Where else should these things be left? And we will take up the note of joyous song in anticipation of the deliverance which will surely come."[1]

CHARLES HADDON SPURGEON IN THE PASTOR IN PRAYER

YIELD YOURSELF TO GOD

In losses, crosses, and troubles, you realize God's presence more conspicuously than ever. The Bible does not say that when you walk along the flowery path or rest on the soft green bank, "I will be with you." It does not say that when you walk on the close cut grass, which feels like a carpet under your feet, "I will be with you." I do not remember reading a Scripture promise like that. But God does say, "When you pass through the waters I will be with you" (Is. 43:2). He gives a special promise for a special time of trial. To meet the doubts of His troubled child, He says, "Fear not, for I have redeemed you; I have called you by your name; you are Mine" (Is. 43:1). Our way to heaven lies through the flood, and through the flood we will go. God has ordained that no trouble, however great, and no persecution, however terrible, will stop the onward march of a soul predestined to eternal joy. Suppose the river is deep and rapid and the torrent sweeps everything before it, still we shall go through it. We shall not be stopped or swept away because God has promised, "When you pass through the waters, I will be with you; and through the rivers, they shall not overflow you (Is. 43:2).[2]

CHARLES HADDON SPURGEON IN BESIDE STILL WATERS

ENJOY HIS PRESENCE

Are you passing through deep, turbulent waters right now in your life? What is the comfort you can take with you as a result of what you've seen in your quiet time with the Lord? Write it out in the space provided and then carry that truth with you throughout the day

Fear not I am with you, O be not dismayed,
For I am your God, I will still give you aid:
I'll strengthen you, help you, and cause you to stand,
Upheld by My gracious, omnipotent hand.
When through the deep waters I call you to go,
The rivers of sorrow will not overflow,
For I will be with you, your trials to bless,
And sanctify to you your deepest distress.
When through fiery trials your pathway shall lie,
My grace all-sufficient shall be your supply
The flames shall not hurt you, I only design
Your dross to consume and your gold to refine.[3]

CHARLES HADDON SPURGEON IN BESIDE STILL WATERS

REST IN HIS LOVE

"Do not be afraid, for I have ransomed you. I have called you by name; you are mine. When you go through deep waters and great trouble, I will be with you. When you go through rivers of difficulty, you will not drown! When you walk through the fire of oppression, you will not be burned up; the flames will not consume you. For I am the LORD, your God, the Holy One of Israel, your Savior" (Isaiah 43:1-3 NLT).

THE DEFINITION OF HOPE

For in hope we have been saved, but hope that is seen is not hope; for who hopes for what he already sees? For if we hope for what we do not see, with perseverance we wait eagerly for it.
ROMANS 8:24-25

PREPARE YOUR HEART

There are times in life when we have what we don't want or want what we don't have. And as a result, it's possible to give in to despair. And then the common refrain is "I have no hope." As a Christian, you can never say you have no hope. You may have no answer in your own mind, but you always have hope. What is hope from God's point of view? That is the subject of your time with the Lord today. As a preparation of heart, draw near to the Lord and pray the words of Psalm 119:18, "Open my eyes, that I may behold wonderful things from your law."

READ AND STUDY GOD'S WORD

1. The Apostle Paul mentions hope at least twelve times in his masterpiece on faith, the book of Romans. Look at the following verses and write everything you learn about hope:

Romans 5:2-5

Romans 8:22-25

2. The Greek word for hope is *elpis* and means "the desire of some good with expectation of obtaining it."[4] Hope is an essential characteristic of the Christian and sets you apart from the world. It is elusive to one who does not know the Lord and unbelievers are left only with a querulous wishing or wanting something to happen. Barclay goes so far as to say that only a Christian can truly be an optimist. Biblical hope is the confidence that knows with certainty the facts, the reality, found in God's Word. God alone gives hope, the ability to hold on to the truth in His

Word, and watch for Him to do something only He can do. Biblical hope is really the highest form of faith—a steadfast certainty based on what God says in His Word. It is not seen except with the eyes of the heart—the eyes of faith. And that is real sight indeed. Hope looks for an answer from God, in His time and in His way. That answer may come in a different form than what you expect. It may be a truth He teaches you from the Bible that sheds new light on your situation. Your circumstance may not change but you will change. You might think of hope as: *Holding On with Patient Expectation.* It is not necessarily the expectation of what God is going to do, but that He is going to do something out of His great plan and purpose. There is always reason to hope because God never stops working in your life. He is never worried or wondering what He is going to do. Nothing is too great or impossible for Him to handle. And He does have a plan and a purpose.

3. As you think about what you have read today, what is the most significant truth you have learned that will help you in life?

ADORE GOD IN PRAYER

Ask the God of hope to give you His hope today. You may wish to turn to the prayer pages in the back of this book and write out those things that are on your heart, lifting each one up to the Lord.

YIELD YOURSELF TO GOD

> "Hope is the ability to listen to the music of the future. Faith is the courage to dance to it in the present."
>
> DR. PETER KUZMIC

> "Have we not known men whose lives have not given out any entrancing music in the day of a calm prosperity, but who, when the tempest drove against them, have astonished their fellows by the power and strength of their music?"[5]
>
> JOHN HENRY JOWETT IN THE SILVER LINING

ENJOY HIS PRESENCE

Dear friend, as you think about all you have learned today, what does it mean, according to God in His Word, to have hope? And then, where in your life are you wanting what you don't have and having what you don't want? Will you take these wishes and desires to the Lord today, lay them at His feet, and then ask Him to give you a new hope according to His promises in His Word? Then, will you Hold On with Patient Expectation and watch what He will do?

REST IN HIS LOVE

"In the morning, O LORD, You will hear my voice; in the morning I will order my prayer to You and eagerly watch" (Psalm 5:3).

THE WAY TO HOPE

For whatever was written in earlier times was written for our instruction, so that through perseverance and the encouragement of the Scriptures we might have hope.

ROMANS 15:4

PREPARE YOUR HEART

Have you ever reached the end of your own strength and thought life as you knew it was over? It's that place where you have no earthly hope and you are on the edge of despair. And then, at the very moment when you could give up, something takes you beyond yourself. Perhaps it is an encouraging word from a friend or a verse in God's Word. That one thing gives you a valiant, courageous heart to say *I cannot give up, no matter what.*

Martin Luther found great courage in the Bible, especially Psalm 46, his favorite psalm in the Bible. It is said that when he would become discouraged and depressed because of the danger and difficulties stemming from the Protestant Reformation, he would turn to his friend and co-worker Philipp Melanchthon and cry out, "Come Philipp, let's sing the 46th Psalm!" As he sang the words of hope from Psalm 46, Luther found the strength to go on in spite of the adversity.

There is a great secret to finding the hope from God that is not dependent on favorable circumstances. And the secret is to open the pages of your Bible and drink in the life-giving water of God's Word. The psalmist has said, "Remember the word to Your servant, in which You have made me hope. This is my comfort in my affliction, that Your word has revived me" (Psalm 119:49-50).

Ask God to bring revival in your heart today from His Word.

READ AND STUDY GOD'S WORD

1. Turn to Romans 15:4 and write this verse out, word-for-word in the space provided.

2. According to this verse, what must you do in order to have hope?

3. Whenever you need hope, open the pages of your Bible. In fact, the next seven weeks will take you on a journey in the Psalms where you will discover the great encouragement God has for you in His Word. Why is God's Word so powerful? Look at the following verses and write out what you learn about the Bible, God's Word:

Isaiah 40:8

Matthew 24:35

John 17:17

2 Timothy 3:16-17

Hebrews 4:12

ADORE GOD IN PRAYER

"Lord, I have thy word my choice,
My lasting heritage;
There shall my noblest powers rejoice,
My warmest thought engage.

I'll read the histories of thy love,

And keep thy laws in sight,

While through the promises I rove,

With ever fresh delight.

Tis a broad land of wealth unknown,

Where springs of life arise,

Seeds of immortal bliss are sown,

And hidden glory lies.

The best relief that mourners have,

It makes our sorrows bless'd;

Our fairest hope beyond the grave,

And our eternal rest."[6]

ISAAC WATTS IN THE PSALMS AND HYMNS OF ISAAC WATTS

YIELD YOURSELF TO GOD

"When all visible evidences that He is remembering us are withheld, that is best; He wants us to realize that His Word, His promise of remembrance, is more substantial and dependable than any evidence of our senses. When He sends the visible evidence that is well also; we appreciate it all the more after we have trusted Him without it."[7]

C.G. TRUMBALL IN STREAMS IN THE DESERT

"Every year, I might almost say every day, that I live, I seem to see more clearly how all the rest and gladness and power of our Christian life hinges on one thing; and that is, taking God at His word, believing that He really means exactly what He says, and accepting the very words in which He reveals His goodness and grace, without substituting others or altering the precise modes and tenses which He has seen fit to use."[8]

FRANCES RIDLEY HAVERGAL IN STREAMS IN THE DESERT

ENJOY HIS PRESENCE

One of the most important decisions you will ever make in life is the place the Word of God will have in your life. Will your Bible sit on a shelf? Will it sit on a table? Will you carry it around once in a while? Or will you open it day by day and will it live in your heart? If you will give time to God and His Word, then dear friend, you are going to overflow with hope, for hope comes from perseverance and the encouragement of the Scriptures (Romans 15:4). Close your time with the Lord by writing a prayer of commitment to Him to spend time with Him each day in His Word.

REST IN HIS LOVE

"I wait for the LORD, my soul does wait, and in His Word do I hope. My soul waits for the Lord more than the watchmen for the morning; indeed, more than the watchmen for the morning" (Psalm 130:5-6).

THE NATURE OF HOPE

Blessed be the God and Father of our Lord Jesus Christ, who according
to His great mercy has caused us to be born again to a living hope
through the resurrection of Jesus Christ from the dead.

1 PETER 1:3

PREPARE YOUR HEART

What does God's kind of hope look like in real life? The words of the hymn, "It Is Well With My Soul," by Horatio Spafford say it best. Will you begin your time with the Lord today meditating on the words he wrote following the death of his four daughters (see the introduction for his story):

When peace like a river attendeth my way,

When sorrows like sea billows roll,

Whatever my lot, Thou hast taught me to say,

"It is well, it is well, with my soul."

Refrain:

It is well, with my soul.

It is well, it is well, with my soul.

My sin - O the bliss of this glorious thought!-

My sin, not in part but the whole,

Is nailed to the cross, and I bear it no more;

Praise the Lord, praise the Lord, O my soul!

Refrain

And Lord, haste the day when the faith shall be sight,

The clouds be rolled back as a scroll,

The trump shall resound, and the Lord shall descend;

"Even so" it is well with my soul.

Refrain.

HORATIO G. SPAFFORD, 1873

READ AND STUDY GOD'S WORD

1. Hope is one of the great hallmarks of the Christian and is a word used throughout the Bible. Many heroes of the Christian faith wrestled with the gravity of their circumstances and found hope in God. Look at the following verses and record what you learn about hope:

Job 13:15 the example of Job

Lamentations 3:21-26 the example of Jeremiah

Romans 5:1-5 the example of Paul

2. Turn to 1 Peter 1:3 and write it out word-for-word.

3. The kind of hope that the Lord gives us is a living hope. And it seems to come to life best in adversity. Where in your life do you need this kind of hope?

ADORE GOD IN PRAYER

Pray the prayer of F.B. Meyer today: "My all is now surrendered to you, my Lord; make of me as much as possible for your glory."[9]

YIELD YOURSELF TO GOD

What can threaten God's existence? Who can oppose His purpose? What can weaken His power? What can dim the clearness of His eye? What can diminish the tenderness of His heart? What can distract the wisdom of His judgment? "You are the same, and Your years will have no end" (Ps. 102:27). Remember, child of God, you are a sheep that can never lose its Shepherd, a child that can never lose its Father. "I will never leave you nor forsake you" (Heb. 13:5), said Jesus as He revealed the Eternal Father's heart. In dire straits, we still have a Father in heaven. A widow had been inconsolable at the loss of her husband, and her little child asked, "Mother, is God dead?" That question rebuked the woman and reminded her that she had a Guardian and Friend. "Your Maker is your husband, the LORD of hosts is His name" (Is. 54:5). Listen, child of God, you can lose your possessions, but you cannot lose your God. Like Jonah, you can see your plant wither (Jon. 4:7), but your God remains. You may lose your land, but not your God. You may lose your savings, but not your Savior. Even if it came to the worst and you were left for a while as one forsaken by God, you still would not lose Him. Like the Lord Jesus on the cross, you may still call Him, "My God" (Matt. 27:46). "'The LORD is my portion,' says my soul, 'therefore I hope in Him'" (Lam. 3:24). The Lord is a portion from which we can never be alienated. He lives! He reigns! He will be our guide even unto death.[10]

CHARLES HADDON SPURGEON IN BESIDE STILL WATERS

ENJOY HIS PRESENCE

As you think about what hope looks like, summarize what you have learned in one or two sentences. Think about why knowing the Lord personally gives you hope. Then, close by thanking the Lord for showing you His truth about hope.

REST IN HIS LOVE

"'The LORD is my portion,' says my soul, 'therefore I have hope in Him.' The LORD is good to those who wait for Him, to the person who seeks Him" (Lamentations 3:24-25).

THE BENEFIT OF HOPE

*This hope we have as an anchor of the soul, a hope both sure
and steadfast and one which enters within the veil.*

HEBREWS 6:19

PREPARE YOUR HEART

Edward Mote never had the benefit of growing up in a godly Christian home but when he was 18 years old he gained the benefit of discovering the hope that God gives those who belong to Him. At that age he was introduced to the Bible and for 37 years he walked with God as a cabinet maker. During this time he began writing hymns. One chorus in particular came to his heart: On Christ the solid Rock I stand, all other ground is sinking sand. By the end of the day he had completed four verses. It was clear he found hope in the Lord—the first line of the first stanza read this way: My hope is built on nothing less than Jesus' blood and righteousness. He pictures a "stormy gale" in life but adds that his anchor will hold: In every high and stormy gale, my anchor holds within the veil. Because there was a time in his life when he didn't even know there was a God, he first entitled his hymn with grand theology, "The Immutable Basis Of A Sinner's Hope." The title was reduced to "The Solid Rock" but it is best known as "My Hope Is Built On Nothing Less." At the age of 55 Edward Mote became a pastor and didn't miss a Sunday for the next 21 years. He was so loved that the congregation offered him title to the church building. He responded, "I do not want the chapel, I only want the pulpit, and when I cease to preach Christ, then turn me out of that."

Edward Mote knew the great hope that God gives and it was an anchor for his soul. Do you know that same hope and is it the anchor for your soul? Begin your time with the Lord today by asking the Lord to give you a heart that hopes in Him.

READ AND STUDY GOD'S WORD

1. Read Hebrews 6:19 and underline every occurrence of the word "hope."

"This hope we have as an anchor of the soul, a hope both sure and steadfast and one which enters within the veil."

2. What do you learn about hope in Hebrews 6:19?

3. As you think about the facts that hope is an anchor, it is sure, it is steadfast, and enters within the veil, the safest place of all in the presence of God Himself, what picture does this give you of hope? Why would such a hope be a great benefit for you in life?

4. How do you need this kind of hope today?

ADORE GOD IN PRAYER

Pray the following prayer from Psalm 31:1-2:

"In You, O LORD, I have taken refuge;
Let me never be ashamed;
In Your righteousness deliver me.
Incline Your ear to me,

rescue me quickly;
Be to me a rock of strength,
A stronghold to save me.
For You are my rock and my fortress;
For Your name's sake You will lead me and guide me."

YIELD YOURSELF TO GOD

My hope is built on nothing less

Than Jesus' blood and righteousness;

I dare not trust the sweetest frame,

But wholly lean on Jesus' name.

Refrain:

On Christ, the solid Rock, I stand;

All other ground is sinking sand,

All other ground is sinking sand.

When darkness veils His lovely face,

I rest on His unchanging grace;

In every high and stormy gale,

My anchor holds within the veil.

Refrain

His oath, His covenant, His blood

Support me in the whelming flood;

When all around my soul gives way,

He then is all my hope and stay.

Refrain

When He shall come with trumpet sound,

Oh, may I then in Him be found;

Dressed in His righteousness alone,

Faultless to stand before the throne.

Refrain

THE SOLID ROCK BY EDWARD MOTE 1797-1874

ENJOY HIS PRESENCE

When you rest your hope on God and His Word you have an anchor for your soul. Every promise, every truth in God's Word is one more tether to your eternal, unchanging God. In the weeks to come you are going to have the opportunity to live in some of the choice promises and truths in all of Scripture—those found in the Psalms. Take some time now to think about what you have learned today and write a prayer to the Lord expressing all that is on your heart.

REST IN HIS LOVE

"Therefore everyone who hears these words of Mine and acts on them, may be compared to a wise man who built his house on the rock. And the rain fell, and the floods came, and the winds blew and slammed against that house; and yet it did not fall, for it had been founded on the rock" (Matthew 7:24-25).

DEVOTIONAL READING
BY CHARLES HADDON SPURGEON

DEAR FRIEND,

The next two days are your opportunity to review what you have learned this week. You may wish to write your thoughts and insights in your Journal. As you think about your study of hope, write:

Your most significant insight:

Your favorite quote:

Your favorite verse:

If the furnace is hot, let your faith be strong. If the burden is heavy, let your patience endure. Acknowledge that He who lends has the right to reclaim. As you bless the giving, bless the taking. There are times when the brightest-eyed Christians can hardly brush the tears away. Strong faith and joyous hope subside into a fear that is scarcely able to keep the spark of hope and faith alive. In times of gloom, when your soul is overwhelmed, grasp the promise and rejoice in the Lord. Although it is not always easy, cry with David, "Why are you cast down, O my soul? And why are you disquieted within me?" (Ps. 42:5). Question the cause of your tears. Reason until you come to the psalmist's conclusion, "Hope in God, for I shall yet praise Him" (Ps. 42:5). If you can believe God in the midnight of your soul, then you have ten times more cause to rejoice than to sorrow. If you can lie humbly at Jesus' feet, there are more flowers than thorns ready to spring up in your path. Joys lie in ambush. You will be surrounded with songs of deliverance. Companions in tribulations, do not give in to hopeless sorrow. Salute with thankfulness…hope, for you shall yet praise Him."[11]

CHARLES HADDON SPURGEON IN BESIDE STILL WATERS

Viewer Guide

What's So Great About Hope?

You have just completed the first week of study in *A Heart That Hopes In God*. Today we are going to share together some devotional thoughts from Hebrews 6:13-19. I want you to see why hope is so valuable for you to have each moment of your life.

"…take hold of the hope set before us. This hope we have as an anchor of the soul, a hope both sure and steadfast and one which enters within the veil…" (Hebrews 6:18-19).

Devotional thoughts from Hebrews 6:13-19

1. God always does what He _____and _____to do. Hebrews 6:17

2. It is _____for God to lie. Hebrews 6:18

3. When God promises something, He _____His promise. Hebrews 6:18

4. He has guaranteed His promise with His _____. He wants you to know He keeps His Word.

5. You have a _____. Hebrews 6:18

Hope is holding on with patient _____.

6. Hope is like an _____. Hebrews 6:19

7. Hope keeps me from _____.
Hebrews 6:19

Why the Psalms are a wonderful place to put your anchor deep into the Word of God

1. Many are written by David, the man after God's own _____.

2. The psalms are our living example of how to have _____in times of difficulty.

3. The psalms are filled with the _____of God.

4. When you anchor your hope in the promises of the Psalms, you will discover that you will not _____.

Practical Applications to take your hope and anchor it in the Psalms:

≈ Video messages are available on DVDs or as Downloadable M4V Video. Audio messages are available on Audio CDs or as Downloadable MP3 Audio. Visit the Quiet Time Ministries Online Store at www.quiettime.org.

Week Two

HOPE WHEN YOU FEEL ALONE

Psalm 139

Hope is patience with the lamp lit.

Tertullian

HE KNOWS ME

O LORD, You have searched me and known me.

PSALM 139:1

PREPARE YOUR HEART

In the darkest night of a trial one of the most desperate experiences is the feeling of solitary aloneness. There is no one who can know the adversity as you do. Behind closed doors who can see, who can really understand what it is that we face in the time of suffering? The answer is that there is One who knows—Jesus. He knows.

In the first century, the churches in western Asia Minor discovered this truth. Jesus appeared to the apostle John and gave him seven letters, one for each of the churches. These churches were facing the fiery trial of persecution from the emperor Domitian. There is a phrase that is repeated at the beginning of each of the seven letters found in Revelation 1-3: I know. Oh what a powerful truth this is to hear from the Creator of the Universe, the One who holds all power in His hand: I know. There is such hope in these words.

As you draw near to the Lord today, ask Him to open your eyes to the hope of the promise that *He knows*.

READ AND STUDY GOD'S WORD

1. This week you will be living in one of the great psalms of the Bible—Psalm 139. The writer of this psalm is David, the shepherd boy who became the King of Israel. The great hallmark of his life, his claim to fame, was that God said this about David: "I have found David, the son of Jesse, a man after My heart, who will do all My will" (Acts 13:22). God called David "a man after My heart." As you read Psalm 139 this week you are going to notice one very important fact about the relationship between God and David—it was intimate. David knew much about the Character and Person of God. How can that be? There is only one way to know your God—spend time with Him. David spent much time alone with God. The result was that he knew things about God that other people did not know. He wrote some of the most profound truths in his journal entries found in many of the psalms in your Bible. Psalm 139, in particular, contains some of the best and highest truths you can know about God. These truths will bring great comfort and hope to you.

Read Psalm 139. What title would you give this psalm?

2. Read Psalm 139:1-6 and write out everything you learn about God.

3. Turn to John 1:43-51 and read this event involving Philip, Nathaniel, and Jesus. How do you think Nathaniel felt when he met Jesus (see especially verses 46-49)?

4. What truth about God brings you the most encouragement today and why?

ADORE GOD IN PRAYER

Pray the words of Psalm 139:1-6 in the New Living Translation to the Lord today thinking about the meaning of each verse for you in your life:

"O LORD, you have examined my heart and know everything about me.
You know when I sit down or stand up.
You know my every thought when far away.
You chart the path ahead of me and tell me where to stop and rest.

Every moment you know where I am.
You know what I am going to say even before I say it, LORD
You both precede and follow me.
You place your hand of blessing on my head.
Such knowledge is too wonderful for me, too great for me to know!"

YIELD YOURSELF TO GOD

Think about the following observations by F.B. Meyer in *Choice Notes In The Psalms* and underline those truths that mean the most to you today:

> *O Lord, you have examined my heart*—What ineffable comfort there is in the thought that our hearts closed to all else, are open to Him…as He can read our secret sorrow, He can apply the healing balm. "He knows all; but loves us better than He knows."

> *When I sit down* is our time of quiet rest; *When I stand up*, the going forth to work. *When far away* perhaps means that God anticipates our thought and purposes before they are matured in our minds.

> *You both precede and follow me*—The All-knowing is also the All-present. We are God-encompassed; God–environed. *Behind*, that none may attack in the rear. *Before*, that He may search out the way and meet our foes. *You place your hand*; as if a child were to put one hand over the hollow of another to keep some frail insect from its pursuer (John 10:28-29).

> *Too wonderful!*—We must worship, where we fail to comprehend.[1]

ENJOY HIS PRESENCE

Have you noticed that God's knowledge of you is not passive as though He is far-off and uncaring. No—God's knowledge of you is personal and active and involved in the details of you. He loves you and desires intimacy with you. Think on these words by A.W. Tozer in The Pursuit of God: "God is a Person, and in the deep of His mighty nature He thinks, wills, enjoys, feels, loves, desires and suffers as any other person may…The continuous and unembarrassed interchange of love and thought between God and the soul of the redeemed man is the throbbing heart of New Testament religion."

Will you draw near to Him today and engage in this most intimate, personal relationship with the Creator of the Universe who loves you? There is a phenomenal promise in James 4:8 for you to ponder as you close your time with the Lord: "Draw near to God and He will draw near to you." And then, when you draw near, you will be able to say along with the psalmist: "But as for me, the nearness of God is my good; I have made the LORD GOD my refuge, that I may tell of all Your works (Psalm 73:28) and How lovely are Your dwelling places, O LORD of hosts!…For a day in Your courts is better than a thousand outside. I would rather stand at the threshold of the house of my God than dwell in the tents of wickedness. For the LORD GOD is a sun and shield; The Lord gives grace and glory; No good thing does He withhold from those who walk uprightly" (Psalm 84:1, 10-11).

Carry the promise of God's presence with you today and know that *He knows*.

REST IN HIS LOVE

"For we do not have a high priest who cannot sympathize with our weaknesses, but One who has been tempted in all things as we are, yet without sin. Therefore let us draw near with confidence to the throne of grace, so that we may receive mercy and find grace to help in time of need" (Hebrews 4:15-16).

HE IS WITH ME

Where can I go from Your Spirit? Or where can I flee from Your presence?
PSALM 139:7

PREPARE YOUR HEART

As you begin your quiet time today, meditate on the words of this prayer from *The Valley Of Vision—A Collection Of Puritan Prayers And Devotions* edited by Arthur Bennett:

"Lord, high and holy, meek and lowly,
Thou hast brought me to the valley of vision,
where I live in the depths but see thee in the heights;
hemmed in by mountains of sin I behold thy glory.
Let me learn by paradox
that the way down is the way up,
that to be low is to be high,
that the broken heart is the healed heart,
that the contrite spirit is the rejoicing spirit,
that the repenting soul is the victorious soul,
that to have nothing is to possess all,
that to bear the cross is to wear the crown,
that to give is to receive,
that the valley is the place of vision.
Lord, in the daytime stars can be seen from deepest wells,
and the deeper the wells the brighter thy stars shine;
Let me find thy light in my darkness,
thy life in my death,
thy joy in my sorrow,
thy grace in my sin,
thy riches in my poverty,
thy glory in my valley."[2]

What is your favorite phrase in this prayer and why?

READ AND STUDY GOD'S WORD

1. Today you are going to think about the magnificent Presence of God in your life and all that it means for you. This is known in theology as the Omnipresence of God. Read Psalm 139:7-12 and write out everything you learn about God.

2. Jesus also gives the comfort and assurance of His Presence with you. Read the following verses and write what you learn:

Matthew 28:18-20

John 14:21-23

Hebrews 13:5

3. What truth means the most to you today?

ADORE GOD IN PRAYER

Pray the words of Psalm 139:7-12 to the Lord, thinking about each verse as you talk with Him.

YIELD YOURSELF TO GOD

What now does the divine immanence mean in direct Christian experience? It means simply that God is here. Wherever we are, God is here. There is no place, there can be no place, where He is not. Ten million intelligences standing at as many points in space and separated by incomprehensible distances can each one say with equal truth, God is here. No point is nearer to God than any other point. It is exactly as near to God from any place as it is from any other place. No one is in mere distance any further from or any nearer to God than any other person is. Our pursuit of God is successful just because He is forever seeking to manifest Himself to us. The revelation of God to any man is not God coming from a distance upon a time to pay a brief and momentous visit to the man's soul. Thus to think of it is to misunderstand it all. The approach of God to the soul or of the soul to God is not to be thought of in spatial terms at all. There is no idea of physical distance involved in the concept. It is not a matter of miles but of experience. To speak of being near to or far from God is to use language in a sense always understood when applied to our ordinary human relationships. A man may say, `I feel that my son is coming nearer to me as he gets older,' and yet that son has lived by his father's side since he was born and has never been away from home more than a day or so in his entire life. What then can the father mean? Obviously he is speaking of experience. He means that the boy is coming to know him more intimately and with deeper understanding, that the barriers of thought and feeling between the two are disappearing, that father and son are becoming more closely united in mind and heart. So when we sing, `Draw me nearer, nearer, blessed Lord,' we are not thinking of the nearness of place, but of the nearness of relationship. It is for increasing degrees of awareness that we pray, for a more perfect consciousness of the divine Presence. We need never shout across the spaces to an absent God. He is nearer than our own soul, closer than our most secret thoughts.[3]

A.W. TOZER IN THE PURSUIT OF GOD

Enjoy His Presence

Do you know this nearness of relationship with God in your own life today? Will you set aside the lesser things and pursue the one great thing—knowing God? If so, then you will experience a hope that is independent of the circumstances of life, one that rests on the very Person and Character of God Himself. You will be able to say with Jeremiah in Lamentations 3:24: "The LORD is my portion, says my soul, Therefore I have hope in Him." Close your time with the Lord by writing a prayer to Him expressing all that is on your heart.

Rest in His Love

"'Lo, I am with you always, even to the end of the age" (Matthew 28:20).

HE CREATED ME

*For You formed my inward parts; You wove me in my mother's womb. I
will give thanks to You, for I am fearfully and wonderfully made;
Wonderful are Your works, and my soul knows it very well.*

PSALM 139:13-14

PREPARE YOUR HEART

She was born in August, 1875, in India and because she was born in so great a year for that
country, the people in her village told her parents she would be great among women. And
so her parents named her Ponnamal, which means "gold". She was to them their great treasure.
As was the custom in India, at the age of nineteen, she was given in marriage to a man who was
a professor in a mission college. Suddenly, after one year, her husband died, and she became a
widow, making her an outcast in the culture of India. Because she had a child, she was taken in by
her in-laws who regarded her with disdain. They tolerated her only for the sake of the child. The
mother-in-law spoke harshly to her from morning to night, daily scolding her for who she was
and all that she did. At first, Ponnamal accepted the ill treatment, wishing for a life of peace and
contentment. But little by little, she sank under it and began to lose her own sense of identity and
self-respect. She was not allowed to wear clean garments or even comb her hair except when she
was taken to church on Sundays. It was felt that this kind of appearance was becoming to a widow.

One evening Ponnamal walked outside, tempted with the idea of throwing herself to the bottom of a well, and giving up on life as so many other widows had before her. Something kept her
from it. And then, something happened that changed everything for this young girl. One day
a missionary couple from the church visited the house where she lived. They were intrigued by
this wild-eyed young girl standing behind a door as they spoke with her in-laws. Ponnamal, very
bright and educated prior to her marriage, listened intently to everything these missionaries shared.
God did a mighty work in her, transforming her on the inside. Realizing she was a child of God,
there was something triumphant and serene in her heart that no one could touch. Her miserable
circumstances were the same, but she was different. She had learned "the secret of possessing that
joy which is not in circumstances, and so does not depend upon them."[4]

One day, a young English missionary woman visited the house and befriended the in-laws.

55

Much to Ponnamal's surprise, this woman requested that the couple allow Ponnamal to go with her on other visits. She was so persistent, that they eventually agreed. That English missionary woman was Amy Carmichael and this is the story of how Ponnamal became her co-laborer in ministry, and thus began the adventures in the missionary work of Dohnavur in India.

Think about this true story of Ponnamal and how God reached out to her in an impossible situation and worked in her life in spite of the stripping of every sense of dignity and respect by her in-laws. No amount of outward trial and devastation can take away the truth of God creating you. He designed you and He loves you. What does He desire more than anything? You. He wants you in a relationship with Him.

Take some time now and ask God to work in your heart today.

READ AND STUDY GOD'S WORD

1. Read Psalm 139:13-15 and write out everything you learn about God.

2. What is most significant to you today from these verses?

3. What does it mean to you to know that God created you?

ADORE GOD IN PRAYER

Meditate on the words of the beloved hymn How Great Thou Art:

O Lord my God, When I in awesome wonder,

Consider all the worlds Thy Hands have made;

I see the stars, I hear the rolling thunder,

Thy power throughout the universe displayed.

Refrain

Then sings my soul, My Saviour God, to Thee,

How great Thou art, How great Thou art.

Then sings my soul, My Saviour God, to Thee,

How great Thou art, How great Thou art!

And when I think, that God, His Son not sparing;

Sent Him to die, I scarce can take it in;

That on the Cross, my burden gladly bearing,

He bled and died to take away my sin.

Refrain

When Christ shall come, with shout of acclamation,

And take me home, what joy shall fill my heart.

Then I shall bow, in humble adoration,

And then proclaim: "My God, how great Thou art!"

Refrain

YIELD YOURSELF TO GOD

God's thorough knowledge of us and all our ways is patent (inherent to, obvious, apparent) from His creative power. Before we breathed, His will arranged our incipient being. What mechanism can be more exquisite in all its parts than the formation of our bodies! Divine skill is manifested in the design of its innumerable members. Wonder is exhausted in the contemplation. Select any part, it proclaims that infinite wisdom devised the plan, and infinite power brought it to perfection. Can this great Creator not have most intimate acquaintance with the being which He thus formed?[5]

HENRY LAW IN DAILY PRAYER AND PRAISE

ENJOY HIS PRESENCE

As you close your time with the Lord today, think about what it means that God is the One who made you, dreamed of you, and desired you for His very own. How does that give you hope today?

REST IN HIS LOVE

"O LORD, how many are Your works! In wisdom you have made them all…" (Psalm 104:24).

HE HAS A PLAN FOR ME

*...in Your book were all written the days that were ordained
for me, when as yet there was not one of them.*

PSALM 139:16

PREPARE YOUR HEART

So often in the darkness of a trial, the sense of purpose becomes clouded over with the dashing of a dream. You had "hoped" for something more and now it appears as though all is lost. Sometimes God will shatter your dreams to broaden your vision. Sometimes the death of a dream is necessary so that you will move away from it to something more than you could have ever imagined. And sometimes the dream has filled the whole landscape of your existence when, in fact, it is God Himself who wants to be your all in all.

Paul encourages you in Romans 12:1-2 with these words: "Therefore I urge you, brethren, by the mercies of God to present your bodies a living and holy sacrifice, acceptable to God, which is your spiritual service of worship. And do not be conformed to this world, but be transformed by the renewing of your mind, so that you may prove what the will of God is, that which is good and acceptable and perfect." And then the writer of Hebrews says this: "Therefore, since we have so great a cloud of witnesses surrounding us, let us also lay aside every encumbrance and the sin which so easily entangles us, and let us run with endurance the race that is set before us, fixing our eyes on Jesus, the author and perfecter of faith..." (Hebrews 12:1-2).

When once you have fixed your focus, your attention on Him, then you are going to discover a new passion in your heart to run your race, that which He sets before you. It may only be a step at a time. And you may be like an Abraham who "went out not knowing where he was going" (Hebrews 11:8). To move on will mean for you a "letting go" and a "surrender" of all that you had in mind and a hearty "yes" to the call of Jesus: follow Me (Matthew 4:19). And then, cling to the promise in Ephesians 3:20-21—"Now to him who is able to do immeasurably more than all we ask or imagine, according to his power that is at work within us, to him be glory in the church and in Christ Jesus throughout all generations for ever and ever! Amen."

Always remember—God has a plan and God has a purpose for you even in the midst of great loss. Knowing He is still at work, carrying out that plan and purpose will give you a hope in Him that will keep you on your course.

READ AND STUDY GOD'S WORD

1. Read the following translations of Psalm 139:16 and underline what is most significant to you today:

> "Your eyes have seen my unformed substance;
> And in Your book were all written
> The days that were ordained for me,
> When as yet there was not one of them." NASB

> "You saw me before I was born.
> Every day of my life was recorded in your book.
> Every moment was laid out
> before a single day had passed." NLT

2. Read the great promise of Jeremiah 29:11 and write out your favorite words from this verse.

3. What does it mean to you today to know that God has a plan for you?

ADORE GOD IN PRAYER

Pray the prayer of Psalm 139:23-24 today:

> "Search me, O God, and know my heart;
> Try me and know my anxious thoughts;
> And see if there be any hurtful way in me,
> And lead me in the everlasting way."

YIELD YOURSELF TO GOD

For when a soul sets out to find God it does not know whither it will come, and by what path it will be led; but those who catch the vision are ready to follow the Lamb whithersoever He goeth, regardless of what that following may involve for them. And it is as they follow, obedient to what they have seen, in this spirit of joyful adventure, that their path becomes clear before them, and they are given the power to fulfil their high calling. They are those who have the courage to break through conventionalities, who care not at all what the world thinks of them, because they are entirely taken up with the tremendous realities of the soul and God.[6]

CHRISTIAN MISSIONARY SOCIETY IN *WHEN GOD CAME*

ENJOY HIS PRESENCE

What is your most significant insight from your quiet time today? What can you take with you that will give you hope and strength to run the race that is set before you?

REST IN HIS LOVE

"For I know the plans that I have for you, declares the LORD, plans for welfare and not for calamity to give you a future and a hope" (Jeremiah 29:11).

HE THINKS ABOUT ME

How precious also are Your thoughts to me, O God! How vast is the sum of them! If I should count them, they would outnumber the sand. When I awake, I am still with You.
PSALM 139:17-18

PREPARE YOUR HEART

Oh, what a week it has been, thinking about these great truths in Psalm 139. They are truths for every soul at every season and stage of life. There is never a time when you do not need to bask in this magnificent truth about God. You always need to know that He knows you intimately, He is with you, He designed you, and He has a plan for you. Today, there is one final truth to think about: God thinks about you. Oh what a powerful promise—to know that He thinks about you. How can that be? There are millions and millions of things for the Lord to think about, but in the midst of it all at all times, He has thought, is thinking, and will think about you. Remember He is God, wholly other, and able to do what man cannot do. He is eternal, self-existent, and all powerful. He spoke the world into existence. This same God is the one who loves you and thinks about you. No wonder the psalmist said, "Such knowledge is too wonderful for me; it is too high, I cannot attain to it" (Psalm 139:6). And even though no human can attain to it or comprehend it all, catching a glimpse transforms the heart and brings hope to light the way.

Begin your quiet time today with the words of Psalm 139:23-24.

> "Search me, O God, and know my heart;
> Try me and know my anxious thoughts;
> And see if there be any hurtful way in me,
> And lead me in the everlasting way."

READ AND STUDY GOD'S WORD

1. Think about the following translations of Psalm 139:17-18 and underline those phrases that are most significant to you today:

"How precious also are Your thoughts to me, O God!
How vast is the sum of them!
If I should count them, they would outnumber the sand.
When I awake, I am still with You." NASB

"How precious are your thoughts about me, O God!
They are innumerable!
I can't even count them; they outnumber the grains of sand!
And when I wake up in the morning you are still with me!" NLT

2. Behind God's thoughts about you is His great love for you. Look at the following verses and write what you learn about God and His love. Personalize your observations and insights.

Isaiah 49:15-16

Jeremiah 31:3

John 3:16

1 John 3:1-3

ADORE GOD IN PRAYER

Draw near to God now and respond to His love and thoughts of you. Talk with Him about all that is on your heart today.

YIELD YOURSELF TO GOD

There is much transport in the knowledge that God thinks on us. If we cannot escape His observant eye, so too we cannot be hid from His vigilant love. He loved

His people before their members were framed, and never has His love relaxed. The value of this knowledge is inestimable, even as the multitude of His thoughts exceed enumeration. The child of God delightedly ponders this truth throughout his waking hours. They attend him until he closes his eyes in nightly repose, and when perception again returns, and the mind resumes its exercise, the same truth continues to gladden.[7]

HENRY LAW IN DAILY PRAYER AND PRAISE

ENJOY HIS PRESENCE

What have you learned from the Lord today that will give you hope? Write out your most significant insight and then carry that thought with you throughout the day.

REST IN HIS LOVE

"Can a woman forget her nursing child and have no compassion on the son of her womb? Even these may forget, but I will not forget you. Behold, I have inscribed you on the palms of My hands; Your walls are continually before me" (Isaiah 49:15-16).

DEVOTIONAL READING
BY AMY CARMICHAEL

DEAR FRIEND,

Take some time now to write about all that you have learned this week. How do these truths give you hope if you feel alone. What has been most significant to you? Close by writing a prayer to the Lord.

What were your most meaningful discoveries this week as you spent time with the Lord?

Most meaningful insight:

Most meaningful devotional reading:

Most meaningful verse:

As you think about all that you have learned this week, meditate on these words by Amy Carmichael: "This, then, is the call to the climbing soul. Expose yourself to the circumstances of His choice, for that is perfect acquiescence in the will of God. We are called to the fellowship of a gallant company. Ye become followers of us, and of the Lord wrote Paul to the men of Thessalonica. Who follows in their train?"

Make me Thy mountaineer;
I would not linger on the lower slope.
Fill me afresh with hope, O God of hope,
That undefeated I may climb the hill
As seeing Him who is invisible,
Whom having not seen I love.
O my Redeemer, when this little while
Lies far behind me and the last defile
Is all alight, and in that light I see
My Saviour and my Lord, what will it be?[8]

AMY CARMICHAEL

Viewer Guide
~ WEEK TWO ~

When God Is Present

In our time together in this message, we are going to look at three strong encouragements from Psalm 139 to help you find hope in life, especially when you may feel as though you are alone.

"O LORD, you have examined my heart and know everything about me. You know when I sit down or stand up. You know my thoughts even when I'm far away. You see me when I travel and when I rest at home. You know everything I do" (Psalm 139:1-3 NLT).

Three things you can know are true no matter what you face in life:

1. God is _____.

Psalm 139:7

Thank You Lord, that You are here.

2. God is _____.

Psalm 139:8

Lord, You hear me and You will respond.

3. God is _____.

Psalm 139:10

Lord, You will help me.

IF ONLY I HAD KNOWN YOU

Lord,
I crawled
  across the barrenness
    to You
    with my empty cup
  uncertain
  in asking
  any small drop
Of refreshment.

If only
I had known You
  better
I'd have come
Running
With a bucket.[9]

NANCY SPIEGELBERG

Video messages are available on DVDs or as Downloadable M4V Video. Audio messages are available on Audio CDs or as Downloadable MP3 Audio. Visit the Quiet Time Ministries Online Store at www.quiettime.org.

Week Three

HOPE WHEN YOU ARE IN TROUBLE

Psalm 31

Before trouble comes, many believers are silent and their heart toward the Lord is heavy, but when providence clips their wings or puts them in a cage, they sing sweetly. Then their faith revives, their hope returns, their love glows, and they sing God's praises in the fire.

CHARLES HADDON SPURGEON

THE FIERY TRIAL

Be gracious to me, O LORD, for I am in distress; my eyes is wasted away from grief,
my soul and my body also. For my life is spent with sorrow and my years with sighing;
My strength has failed because of my iniquity, and my body has wasted away.
PSALM 31:9-10

PREPARE YOUR HEART

When a trial is truly a trial, the fire is hot and the first instinct is to run or do something to change the circumstance. Frustration and despair knock on the door of both heart and mind when there is seemingly "nothing you can do." All control and possible change of the circumstance is seemingly taken out of one's hand. Is there any hope in the fiery trial?

Annie Johnson Flint was just such a one who faced this very fire of a trial. She had the dream to be a composer and a concert pianist. At the age of nine she discovered that she could put words together in rhythm and rhyme. At the age of twelve she began setting her poems to music. At the age of fourteen she was stricken with arthritis and within five years was unable to walk. Her condition made it impossible to play the piano. And so she turned her whole attention to the writing of poetry. She saw in her writing the work and ministry that God had called her to from the very beginning. The beauty and power of what she has written comes out of the crucible of the fiery trial, her experience with the Word of God, and the unseen reality of the presence of God Himself. Her pain was so great that pillows were placed around her room to provide a bit of comfort as she leaned carefully and slowly on them. And yet, the unseen spiritual realities she knew from the Word of God were so much greater than her pain that her poetry sings of profound truth giving hope in the most desperate of circumstances.

Are you facing the trial that is "truly a trial" today? Will you turn to the Lord now and ask Him to open your eyes to a reality, a truth from His Word that will fill your heart with overflowing hope?

READ AND STUDY GOD'S WORD

1. This week you are going to live in Psalm 31, a psalm for those who are in a fiery trial. It's for those who need hope in the midst of some kind of trouble. It could be any kind of trouble—emotional, physical, spiritual. It's something where you don't have the resources, in and of your-

self, to handle. It's something greater than you and looms large on the landscape of your life. The author of this psalm is David, the man after God's own heart. He was facing just such a trial. He had been anointed by the prophet, Samuel, to be the next king of God's people, the people of Israel. And yet, in the Lord's economy of perfect timing, plan and purpose, God did not place him in the position of king right away. In fact, David had to wait many years for the fruition of God's promise to be king. Not only that, he had to run for his very life as King Saul chased after him to hunt him down and kill him. Just imagine what it would be like to have to find places to hide from the most powerful man on the earth. At one point we know that David became very discouraged. He said, "How long O LORD? Will You forget me forever? How long will You hide Your face from me?" (Psalm 13:1). But there is no such despair seen in the writing of Psalm 31. While he is experiencing grief, distress and sorrow in the trial, there is a thread of hope. Today, in preparation for your week of quiet times, will you turn to Psalm 31 and read through these words written by David, keeping in mind what you now know about the background of the psalm? Look for the thread of hope in this powerful psalm.

2. As you read Psalm 31, what was most significant to you? Write your thoughts and insights.

ADORE GOD IN PRAYER

Pray the prayer of Psalm 31:1-2 today remembering that "This is the confidence which we have before Him, that if we ask anything according to His will, He hears us. And if we know that He hears us in whatever we ask, we know that we have the requests which we have asked from Him" (1 John 5:14-15). Praying the Word of God is very powerful because His Word reveals His will.

> "In You, O LORD, I have taken refuge;
> Let me never be ashamed;
> In Your righteousness deliver me.
> Incline Your ear to me, rescue me quickly;
> Be to me a rock of strength,
> A stronghold to save me."

YIELD YOURSELF TO GOD

> God hath not promised skies always blue,
> flower-strewn pathways all our lives through;
> God hath not promised sun without rain,
> Joy without sorrow, peace without pain.
>
> But God hath promised strength for the day,
> rest for the labor, light for the way,
> grace for the trials, help from above,
> unfailing sympathy, undying love.[1]

ANNIE JOHNSON FLINT IN BEST-LOVED POEMS

ENJOY HIS PRESENCE

What trial are you facing today? How does what you have learned from Annie Johnson Flint and David in Psalm 31 give you a glimmer of hope based on these spiritual truths and realities? Write your thoughts in the space provided.

REST IN HIS LOVE

"Beloved, do not be surprised at the fiery ordeal among you, which comes upon you for your testing, as though some strange thing were happening to you; but to the degree that you share the sufferings of Christ, keep on rejoicing, so that also at the revelation of His glory you may rejoice with exultation" (1 Peter 4:12-13).

ANATOMY OF A TRIAL

I am forgotten as a dead man, out of mind; I am like a broken vessel.
PSALM 31:12

PREPARE YOUR HEART

Have you ever felt forgotten, as though there is not a single person on the earth who knows about you or even thinks of you? Have you ever felt as David did, like a broken vessel? That, dear friend, is the nature of a trial when it is really a trial. Peter says, "Beloved, do not be surprised at the fiery ordeal among you, which comes upon you for your testing, as though some strange thing were happening to you…" (1 Peter 4:12). The trial that is truly a trial is often fiery and seems strange. It is strange because it is foreign, alien and does not seem like something that would happen to one who belongs to God. Whenever you think of that, always think of Jesus. The journey of Jesus included the cross. And in the garden of Gethsemane, Jesus pleaded with God to remove the cup from Him. He said this to the Father: "Father, if You are willing, remove this cup from Me; yet not My will, but Yours be done" (Luke 22:42). You can know that Jesus walked the road of the fiery trial.

Vreni Schiess says this about trials: "Tribulation is that which makes us chafe, feel pressured and burdened. It is what we long to throw off, escape from, kiss goodbye once and for all—even if it is only drudgery of work or the sheer cussedness of mechanical marvels that keep breaking down. Tribulation is the swamp we want to cross in a hurry to get to the field we hope to leisurely cultivate for a luxuriant growth of faith. But Jesus cautions that we will always be swamped with trials large and small and that our investment of faith begins and ends precisely there."[2]

Our faith grows in the trial. And therein lies the encouragement. There is a purpose to this trial and faith in God is at work in you. And with the Lord there is always light at the end of the tunnel. Did you know that even Jesus found hope from Psalm 31—He actually quoted Psalm 31:5 while on the cross, "Into Your hand I commit my spirit" (Luke 23:46). If He found hope, then you can too.

Today, ask God to speak to the deepest needs in your heart from His Word. This is a very important prayer because there are needs in you that you don't even know—but God knows and He will meet them with Himself.

READ AND STUDY GOD'S WORD

1. Yesterday you began your journey in Psalm 31. Write out in your own words the background of this Psalm answering the question, "Who is the author and what are his circumstances?"

2. Read Psalm 31 and list everything you learn about the author's circumstances based on what he says in this psalm.

3. Describe in your own words the nature of David's trial including his feelings and circumstances.

4. What is the most difficult for you when you experience a trial in your own life?

ADORE GOD IN PRAYER

Pray the prayer of Psalm 31:7-8 to the Lord today:

"I will rejoice and be glad in Your lovingkindness,
 Because You have seen my affliction;
 You have known the troubles of my soul,
 and You have not given me over into the hand of the enemy;
 You have set my feet in a large place."

YIELD YOURSELF TO GOD

Sometimes a light surprises
The Christian while he sings;
It is the Lord who rises
With healing in His wings;
When comforts are declining,
He grants the soul again
A season of clear shining,
To cheer it after rain.

Though vine nor fig-tree neither
Their wonted fruit should bear;
Though all the field should wither,
Nor flocks nor herds be there,
Yet, God the same abiding,
His praise shall tune my voice,
For, while in Him confiding,
I cannot but rejoice.

WILLIAM COWPER 1731-1800

ENJOY HIS PRESENCE

Always know and be assured that what is happening to you when you face trouble is part of the experience of adversity for every child of God. This doesn't change the intensity of your trial, but it does help you to persevere when you know that God is not surprised about it and that He is not wondering what He is going to do. Take comfort in the words of Jesus today, "These things I have spoken to you, so that in Me you may have peace. In the world you have tribulation, but take courage; I have overcome the world" (John 16:33). John says, "For whatever is born of God overcomes the world; and this is the victory that has overcome the world—our faith. Who is the one who overcomes the world, but he who believes that Jesus is the Son of God" (1 John 5:4-5). Vreni Schiess says, "If in God's economy we pay a price for sharing His visions, we also win the prize of tasting His victories."[3] The great victory we can look to is the victory of Christ in His death on the cross and in His resurrection. As Corrie ten Boom used to always say, "Jesus is Victor." Oh what hope there is in that today!

REST IN HIS LOVE

"But in all these things we overwhelmingly conquer through Him who loved us. For I am convinced that neither death, nor life, nor angels, nor principalities, nor things present, nor things to come, no powers, nor height, nor depth, nor any other created thing, will be able to separate us from the love of God, which is in Christ Jesus our Lord" (Romans 8:37-39).

AN ALTERNATE VIEW OF THE TRIAL

But as for me, I trust in You, O LORD, I say, "You are my God." My times are in Your hand…

PSALM 31:14-15

PREPARE YOUR HEART

What do you do when faced with difficulties in life? There are some who are giving up at the least hint of an adversity. And there are others who are faced with devastating circumstances and yet they are hanging in there by faith. What makes the difference? Perspective. And more specifically, it is an eternal perspective that makes all the difference. The eternal perspective is *the ability to see all of life from God's point of view and have what you see affect how you live in the present.*[4] The eternal perspective is found in the Bible, God's Word. There one can discover all that is true and calculate those truths from God into a response to the circumstance. Then, one is ruled by truth rather than feelings and circumstances. It does not mean we don't grieve or mourn. It doesn't mean that we don't feel pain and brokenness. What it does mean is that those truths and promises will give you the ability to see beyond the pain and experience that ability to *Hold On with Patient Expectation*. Here are just a few truths about your trials. They are truths to bring you hope in the trial. Meditate on them as you begin your quiet time today with the Lord. Underline those phrases in each verse that mean the most to you.

- "Weeping may last through the night, but joy comes with the morning." Psalm 30:5 NLT

- "We can rejoice, too, when we run into problems and trials, for we know that they help us develop endurance. And endurance develops strength of character, and character strengthens our confident hope of salvation. And this hope will not lead to disappointment. For we know how dearly God loves us, because he has given us the Holy Spirit to fill our hearts with his love." Romans 5:3-5 NLT

- "For his Spirit joins with our spirit to affirm that we are God's children. And since we are his children, we are his heirs. In fact, together with Christ we are heirs of God's glory. But if we are to share his glory, we must also share his suffering. Yet

what we suffer now is nothing compared to the glory he will reveal to us later."
Romans 8:16-18 NLT

• "That is why we never give up. Though our bodies are dying, our spirits are being renewed every day. For our present troubles are small and won't last very long. Yet they produce for us a glory that vastly outweighs them and will last forever! So we don't look at the troubles we can see now; rather, we fix our gaze on things that cannot be seen. For the things we see now will soon be gone, but the things we cannot see will last forever." 2 Corinthians 4:16-18 NLT

• "Dear brothers and sisters, when troubles come your way, consider it an opportunity for great joy. For you know that when your faith is tested, your endurance has a chance to grow. So let it grow, for when your endurance is fully developed, you will be perfect and complete, needing nothing." James 1:3-4 NLT

• "So be truly glad. There is wonderful joy ahead, even though you have to endure many trials for a little while. These trials will show that your faith is genuine. It is being tested as fire tests and purifies gold—though your faith is far more precious than mere gold. So when your faith remains strong through many trials, it will bring you much praise and glory and honor on the day when Jesus Christ is revealed to the whole world." 1 Peter 1:6-7 NLT

READ AND STUDY GOD'S WORD

1. Psalm 31 is filled with truths that will give you hope. There was a reason why David said in Psalm 31:14 "But as for me, I trust in You, O LORD." Even though he was chased for years on end by King Saul, David was able to say in the darkness and desperation, "as for me, I trust in You, O LORD." Read Psalm 31 and write out every truth and promise that gave David hope including what David knew to be true about God.

2. What truth did you see that gives you the greatest hope today and why?

ADORE GOD IN PRAYER

Open my eyes, that I may see
glimpses of truth Thou hast for me;
place in my hands the wonderful key
that shall unclasp and set me free.
Silently now I wait for Thee,
ready, my God, Thy will to see;
open my eyes—illumine me, Spirit divine!

Open my ears, that I may hear
voices of truth Thou sendest clear;
and while the wave-notes fall on my ear,
ev'rything false will disappear.
Silently now I wait for Thee,
ready, my God, Thy will to see;
open my ears—illumine me, Spirit divine!

Open my mouth, and let me bear
gladly the warm truth ev'rywhere.
Open my heart and let me prepare

love with Thy children thus to share.

Silently now I wait for Thee,

ready, my God, Thy will to see;

open my heart—illumine me, Spirit divine!

CLARA SCOTT 1841-1897

YIELD YOURSELF TO GOD

Faith is the spiritual spy of the soul. It travels far into the promised land, gathers the ripe clusters—the evidences and earnest of its reality and richness...Ah! many a glimpse and gleam of the heavenly land dawns upon the Christian in the darkness of his dungeon, in the loneliness of his exile, in the cloistered stillness of his suffering chamber...Earth shall not always be our place of exile; we shall not always sing the Lord's song in a strange land, nor always shed these tears and wear these fetters and endure these cruel taunts of our foes. Each trembling step of faith, each holy aspiration of love, each sin subdued, each foe vanquished, each trial past, each temptation baffled, is bringing us nearer and still nearer to the bright threshold of glory...⁵

OCTAVIUS WINSLOW IN HELP HEAVENWARD

ENJOY HIS PRESENCE

You have seen many powerful truths today. These truths are His eternal perspective. God transforms us from the inside out as He takes truth from his Word and changes the way we think (see Romans 12:2). What truth did you see today that gives you hope in the midst of your circumstances in life? What will change in how you respond in your circumstance? Write your thoughts and then close in prayer thanking the Lord for speaking to you from His Word.

REST IN HIS LOVE

"Now faith is the assurance of the things we hope for, the proof of the reality of the things we cannot see" (Hebrews 11:1 WMS).

THE SECRET PLACE IN THE TRIAL

You hide them in the secret place of Your presence from the conspiracies of man; You keep them secretly in a shelter from the strife of tongues.

PSALM 31:20

PREPARE YOUR HEART

So often in times of trouble the first inclination is to run away. You need to know, as God's child, that there is a place to run. You can run to "the secret place" of God's Presence. The secret place of His Presence is a shelter for you according to Psalm 31:20. It means that when you run to God, He is your protective covering, a hiding place for you in the storms of life. Today you are going to think about what it means to run to God and find the "secret place" of His Presence. Draw near to Him now and ask Him to speak to you in His Word.

READ AND STUDY GOD'S WORD

1. The Lord is a shelter for you in times of trouble. He is the place where you can run and find comfort in the storm. The best way to run to Him is to find a quiet place, open your Bible, and read and think about what He says in His Word. You might write your thoughts in your journal or in your quiet time notebook. Find some good devotional books that open up the Word of God to you in a way that you can more readily understand what He is saying to you. Some of the best devotional reading is by A.W. Tozer, Oswald Chambers, Andrew Murray, Amy Carmichael, Mrs. Charles Cowman, and F.B. Meyer. Talk with Him about all that is on your heart. Your quiet time is the place where you will find shelter in the Lord and the quiet place of His Presence.[6]

2. The Lord as your shelter and secret place to run is a truth found throughout Scripture. Look at the following verses and write out what you learn.

Psalm 31:8

Psalm 32:7

85

Psalm 46:1

Psalm 119:114

3. Why do you think God's Presence is called a "secret" place and what benefit can there be in running to the secret place of His Presence? Write your thoughts in the space provided.

ADORE GOD IN PRAYER

"Lord, Thou hast said that our Father in heaven notes even the fall of a sparrow to the ground. Help us to believe, O God, that Thou art concerned not only with the rolling of the spheres in their orbits, but even with each of us, our doubts, and perplexities. We remember all too well the bitter discoveries we have made when we have tried to run our lives our own way, when we try to steer our own craft. Wilt Thou come aboard, Lord Jesus, and set us a true course, for we grow weary of life's demands, tired of our own blundering ways. We seek a clear light to shine upon our troubled way. We ask Thee to give us clearer directions. Where we have missed the way and wandered far, bring us back at whatever cost to our pride. Take away our stubborn self-will, for we know that in Thy will alone is our peace. We seek that peace. We pray in that name which is above every name, even Jesus Christ our Lord. Amen."[7]

PETER MARSHALL IN THE PRAYERS OF PETER MARSHALL

YIELD YOURSELF TO GOD

In the secret place of Thy presence—What a compensation for slandered saints! Perhaps we never know that hiding until we have tasted the proud hatred and contempt of man. Do you know the royal withdrawing room? God's pavilion is sound-tight; the strife of tongues cannot invade.[8]

F.B. MEYER IN CHOICE NOTES ON THE PSALMS

ENJOY HIS PRESENCE

Don't you love thinking about the secret place of His presence as the "royal withdrawing room" as F.B. Meyer has called it! Will you run to the royal withdrawing room today to meet with your Lord? If so, you will find a new strength and a new courage and a new hope to face the day.

REST IN HIS LOVE

"You are my refuge and my shield; your word is my source of hope" (Psalm 119:114 NLT).

HIS MARVELOUS LOVINGKINDNESS IN THE TRIAL

Blessed be the LORD, for He has made marvelous His lovingkindness to me in a besieged city.
PSALM 31:21

PREPARE YOUR HEART

In God's economy, certain truths seem contrary to the natural world. How can any good come from something tumultuous and painful in life? And yet, God promises it over and over again. And if He continues to say it, then we must at some point, begin perhaps dimly at first, then wholeheartedly embrace what He says and apply it to our wounded heart. David's experience is written for all to see. And his firsthand account of what God has done in his time of trouble is here in plain language. David says, "He has made marvelous His lovingkindness to me in a besieged city" (Psalm 31:21). David's trouble brought out new and marvelous expressions of God's love in his life. But you are going to see that David is called the man after God's own heart for a reason. David responded in certain ways in the midst of his trouble and it enabled him to experience the love of God in an intimate relationship with Him.

READ AND STUDY GOD'S WORD

1. Read through Psalm 31 again and write out all the responses of David in the midst of his trouble.

2. One of his responses was to draw near to God in prayer. He says in Psalm 31:22, "As for me, I said in my alarm, I am cut off from before Your eyes; nevertheless You heard the voice of my supplications." Think about these specific prayer requests of David in Psalm 31 and underline your favorite phrases in each one:

"Let me never be ashamed. In Your righteousness deliver me." Psalm 31:1

"Incline Your ear to me, rescue me quickly; be to me a rock of strength, a stronghold to save me." Psalm 31:2

"Be gracious to me, O Lord, for I am in distress…" Psalm 31:9

"Deliver me from the hand of my enemies and from those who persecute me." Psalm 31:15

"Make Your face to shine upon Your servant; Save me in Your lovingkindness." Psalm 31:16

"Let me not be put to shame, O LORD, for I call upon You; let the wicked be put to shame, let them be silent in Sheol. Let the lying lips be mute, which speak arrogantly against the righteous with pride and contempt." Psalm 31:17-18

3. Of course, most of Psalm 31 is directed to God. Do you notice how easy it is for David to talk with God? He and God had an intimate love relationship where David experienced God's lovingkindness in "marvelous" ways especially when he was in trouble. That word "marvelous" is *paia* in Hebrew and means extraordinary, astonishing, wonderful, and miraculous. In this case, what David was saying is that when he was in trouble he saw God's expression of love to him as beyond the bounds of human powers or expectations.[9] And was this not true? Think about how Jonathan, the son of Saul, warned David to run because his life was in danger. Think of how David, as a young man, was able to kill the giant Goliath with a sling and stones. David saw God do what no man could do. And in Psalm 31 David saw God as a refuge, a deliverer, a rock of strength, a stronghold, a fortress, and his strength. What incredible expressions of the lovingkindness of God. As you think about what you have seen in your quiet time, how did David's trial enable him to experience the extraordinary, astonishing lovingkindness of God?

4. How did David's response in his trial impact his experience of the love of God?

ADORE GOD IN PRAYER

Pray the prayer of David today from Psalm 31:16. "Make Your face to shine upon Your servant; save me in Your lovingkindness."

YIELD YOURSELF TO GOD

> I stood on the shore beside the sea;
> The wind from the West blew fresh and free,
> While past the rocks at the harbor's mouth
> The ships went North, and the ships went South,
> And some sailed out on an unknown quest,
> And some sailed into the harbor's rest;
> Yet ever the wind blew out of the West.
>
> I said to one who had sailed the sea
> That this was a marvel unto me;
> For how can the ships go safely forth,
> Some to the South and some to the North,
> Far out to sea on their golden quest,
> Or in to the harbor's calm and rest,
> And ever the wind blew out of the West?
>
> The sailor smiled as he answered me,
> "Go where you will when you're on the sea,
> Though head winds baffle and flaws delay,
> You can keep the course by night and day,

Drive with the breeze or against the gale;
It will not matter what winds prevail,
For all depends on the set of the sail."

Voyager soul on the sea of life,
O'er waves of sorrow and sin and strife,
When fogs bewilder and foes betray,
Steer straight on your course from day to day;
Though unseen currents run deep and swift,
Where rocks are hidden and sandbars shift,
All helpless and aimless, you need not drift.

Oh, set your sail to the heavenly gale,
And then, no matter what winds prevail,
No reef shall wreck you, no calm delay,
No mist shall hinder, no storm shall stay;
Though far you wander and long you roam,
Through salt sea-spray and o'er white sea-foam,
No wind that can blow but shall speed you home.[10]

ANNIE JOHNSON FLINT IN BEST-LOVED POEMS

ENJOY HIS PRESENCE

Dear friend, have you set your sail today in such a way that in the trouble you are sailing on the ocean of God's love? Have you run to Him? Are you crying out to Him? Octavius Winslow says "there is no help heavenward like unto prayer and no ladder the rungs of which will bring you so near to God as prayer."[11] Take encouragement from the final words of David in this psalm: "O love the LORD, all you His godly ones! The LORD preserves the faithful and fully recompenses the proud doer. Be strong and let your heart take courage, all you who hope in the Lord" (Psalm 31:23-24). God bless you as you continue to draw near to Him. Close by writing a prayer in your journal expressing all that is on your heart.

REST IN HIS LOVE

"Yes we know that all things go on working together for the good of those who keep on loving God, who are called in accordance with God's purpose" (Romans 8:28 WMS).

DEVOTIONAL READING
BY OCTAVIUS WINSLOW

DEAR FRIEND,

The next two days are your opportunity to review what you have learned this week. Write a prayer to the Lord thanking Him for all He is teaching you about hope.

As you think about how to find hope when you are in trouble, record:

Most meaningful insight:

Most meaningful devotional reading:

Most meaningful verse:

There are few things in the spiritual history of the child of God more really helpful heavenward than sanctified trial. He treads no path in which he finds aid more favourable to advancement in the divine life...Sweet are the uses of adversity to an heir of heaven. Its form may appear ugly and venomous for no chastening for the present seemeth to be joyous, but grievous; nevertheless it bears a precious jewel in its head, for afterward it yieldeth the peacable fruit of righteousness unto them which are exercised thereby (Hebrews 12:11). Affliction is to the believer what the wing is to the lark and what the eye is to the eagle, the means by which the soul mounts in praise heavenward, gazing closely and steadily upon the glorious Sun of righteousness…Trial quickens us in prayer, and so effectually helps us heavenward. The life of God in the soul on earth is a life of communion of the soul with God in heaven…Oh, what a sacred and precious privilege is this![12]

OCTAVIUS WINSLOW IN HELP HEAVENWARD

Viewer Guide

Looking Down From The Top

In a time of trouble it's helpful to move to a higher elevation and get the vertical view. We are going to look at Psalm 31 together and talk about how to have the eternal perspective in the fiery trials of life. So grab your Bible, and let's get into the Word of God together.

"I will rejoice and be glad in Your lovingkindness, because You have seen my affliction; You have known the troubles of my soul, and You have not given me over into the hand of the enemy; You have set my feet in a large place" (Psalm 31:7-8).

The eternal perspective is the ability to see all of life from _____point of view and have what you see affect how you _____in the present.

2 Corinthians 4:17-18

There are two views: what is_____and what is_____.

Three encouragements from Psalm 31 when you are in a time of trouble:

1. The Lord can be _____. Therefore, _____
yourself into His hands. Psalm 31:5-6

2. The Lord _____you. Therefore, there is something to
_____and be glad about.

Psalm 31:7

3. Your _____are in the Lord's _____,
therefore _____to Him in your trouble.

Psalm 31:15

How do we look down from the top?

The secret is found in the _____ of God.

> "My life is but a weaving between my God and me.
> I do not choose the colors, he worketh steadily.
> Ofttimes he weaveth sorrow, and I in foolish pride,
> Forget he sees the upper, and I the underside.
> Not till the loom is silent and the shuttles cease to fly,
> Will God unroll the canvas and explain the reason why.
> The dark threads are as needful in the skillful weaver's hand,
> As the threads of gold and silver in the pattern he has planned."
>
> CORRIE TEN BOOM

Video messages are available on DVDs or as Downloadable M4V Video. Audio messages are available on Audio CDs or as Downloadable MP3 Audio. Visit the Quiet Time Ministries Online Store at www.quiettime.org.

Week Four

HOPE WHEN YOU ARE DISCOURAGED

Psalm 18

Never give up, for that is just the place and time when the tide will turn.

HARRIET BEECHER STOWE

WHO DO I LOVE?

I love you, Lord; you are my strength.
PSALM 18:1 NLT

PREPARE YOUR HEART

G. Campbell Morgan was probably the most widely popular Bible teacher of his day. And that is saying something when you realize that he was in the company of such greats as F.B. Meyer, A.C. Gaebelein, W.H. Griffith Thomas, Charles Erdman, C.I. Scofield, A.T. Pierson, and others. He crossed the ocean over 50 times to teach the Bible and was wildly popular at Moody's summer Bible conferences in Northfield, Massachusetts. G. Campbell Morgan never attended seminary. But he was a student of the Bible. He was preaching by the age of sixteen, but at the age of twenty experienced a crisis of the heart. Because of the popular writings of Darwin and Huxley, he began to question the authority of Scripture. He confronted his crisis head-on, took all of his books and locked them in a cupboard, went to the corner bookstore and bought a new Bible, and went home and locked himself in his room; finally, alone with God and the Word. "Of this I am sure," he said, "if it be the Word of God, and if I come to it with an unprejudiced and open mind, it will bring assurance to my soul of itself."[1] His searching lasted two years but he emerged with such a conviction of heart and a love for the Lord that his preaching cut through countless doubts and drew thousands to the heart of God.

The discouragement of G. Campbell Morgan and the heart crisis he experienced was answered by opening the pages of the Bible and living there. The result was an immovable faith and love for Christ. He describes it this way: "That Bible found me...I have been a student ever since and still am."

If you find yourself discouraged, and you are ready to give up, will you ask God to reveal Himself in His Word today? His Word will produce a new love and worship and devotion in your heart (Psalm 119:38). Begin your quiet time by writing a prayer expressing all that is on your heart.

READ AND STUDY GOD'S WORD

1. Psalm 18 is one of the longer psalms in the Bible and is filled with rich nuggets of gold. Oh what treasure is found here. Variations of this psalm are found in 2 Samuel 22. It was written by David in response to God's deliverance of him from the hand of "all his enemies and from the hand of Saul" (information in the psalm title). David experienced three great deliverances: from the hand of King Saul during the many years David had to hide from him in the wilderness, from the hand of Israel's enemies, and from the hand of his son Absalom. James Montgomery Boice calls Psalm 18 a thanksgiving song and a kingship psalm, rehearsing God's many blessings on the king. It is a song that can be sung by anyone who has experienced the blessing and deliverance of God. Spurgeon gives it the title, The Grateful Retrospect. Read Psalm 18 in one sitting. What title would you give this psalm? Write it out in the space provided.

2. Read Psalm 18:1-2 and write everything you learn about God from these verses. Underline your favorite insight from these verses.

3. David says "I love you, O Lord, my strength." That word for love is *raham* and means to love deeply and compassionately. It is used only once in all of Scripture in the Qal verb form here in Psalm 18:1 of the love of man toward God—in this case, David's tender, affectionate love for God—and elsewhere is used of the love God has for man. What does this tell you about David's relationship with God?

4. What do you think is required to have the kind of intimate, tender, love relationship with God that is apparent in David's life?

ADORE GOD IN PRAYER

Pray the words of F.B. Meyer today: "May I love you, my God and Father, with a holy, absorbing, and increasing love, not for what you give, but for who you are."[2]

YIELD YOURSELF TO GOD

God is never in a hurry but spends years with those He expects to greatly use. He never thinks the days of preparation too long or too dull. The hardest ingredient in suffering is often time. A short, sharp pain is easily borne, but when a sorrow drags its weary way through long, monotonous years, and day after day returns with the same dull routine of hopeless agony, the heart loses its strength, and without the grace of God, is sure to sink into the very sullenness of despair. Joseph's was a long trial (Genesis 39-45), and God often has to burn His lesson into the depths of our being by the fires of protracted pain. *He shall sit as a refiner and purifier of silver*, but He knows how long, and like a true goldsmith He stops the fires the moment He sees His image in the glowing metal. We may not see now the outcome of the beautiful plan which God is hiding in the shadow of His hand; it yet may be long concealed; but faith may be sure that He is sitting on the throne, calmly waiting the hour when, with adoring rapture, we shall say, *all things have worked together for good*. Like Joseph, let us be more careful to learn all the lessons in the school of sorrow than we are anxious for the hour of deliverance. There is a need-be for every lesson, and when we are ready, our deliverance will surely come, and we shall find that we could not have stood in our place of higher service without the very things that were taught us in the ordeal. God is educating us for the future, for higher service and nobler blessings; and if we have the qualities that fit us for a throne, nothing can keep us from it when God's time has come. Don't steal tomorrow out of God's hands. Give God time to speak to you and reveal His will. He is never too late; learn to wait.[3]

MRS. CHARLES COWMAN IN STREAMS IN THE DESERT

ENJOY HIS PRESENCE

Think about all that David needed to become in character and commitment to be God's king over the people of Israel. The trials surely sharpened his character. Discouragement often comes in the longevity of the trial. Surely David knew this longevity in his great need for multiple deliverances throughout his life. More than once he said, "How long, O Lord?" Moses knew the lengthy trial in his 40 years of wilderness wandering and Abraham in his call from God and subsequent journeys in the wilderness. Hope dawns when the eyes turn to God. A realization is borne in the heart of one who comes to know the Person and Works of God in a new and deeper way. In the day of discouragement the greatest "first thing" to do is to renew your vows to the Lord and revive your love for Him. Acts 3:19 tells you that "times of refreshing come from the presence of the Lord." Take some time and just bask in His presence. How exactly can you do that? First, find a quiet place. You may want to go to a park or the mountains. Or find an obscure booth in one of your favorite restaurants. Or go to your local public library. Then, gather some quiet time materials together such as a quiet time notebook or journal, devotional reading, a good deep book with thought-provoking material such as *Knowing God* by J.I. Packer, worship music, word study tools such as *The Key Word Study Bible*, a one volume commentary, and/or Bible study software such as Scholar's Library by Logos.

As David thought about his life and how God had delivered him from King Saul, his first reflection was his love for the Lord. David had a heart for God. This kept him going in the face of a thousand discouragements. And your heart for the Lord will keep you in the race of life as well. Always remember James 4:8, "Draw near to God and He will draw near to you." Close your time with God today by writing a prayer to Him expressing all that is on your heart.

REST IN HIS LOVE

"Establish Your word to Your servant, as that which produces reverence for You" (Psalm 119:38).

WHO DO I CALL?

I called on the LORD, who is worthy of praise, and he saved me from my enemies…But in my distress I cried out to the LORD; yes, I prayed to my God for help. He heard me from his sanctuary; my cry to him reached his ears.

PSALM 18:3, 6 NLT

PREPARE YOUR HEART

Have you learned the secret of crying out to the Lord in your discouragement? David had a habit of always asking God and calling on him for everything he faced in life. The greatest example of this is seen in David's psalms he has written and are in the Bible. Most of them are prayers to the Lord. Notice when you read the psalms of David that he easily moves from talking about God to talking to God. It is said that Corrie ten Boom did the same thing. She would sit at the table with a group of people and while talking with them about something she would turn her gaze to the Lord and respond to Him or make a comment to Him. It was as though He was so very present in Corrie's life that it would have been impolite to ignore Him. Have you cultivated just such a relationship? Do you know that natural exchange of conversation with your Lord so that when you are in distress, discouraged, or troubled, the first One you talk with is your Lord? Will you ask Him now to give you this rare privilege of communion and comaraderie and companionship with Him?

READ AND STUDY GOD'S WORD

1. Oh, what a privilege it is to call out to God in your greatest times of need. Read Psalm 18:3-6. Answer the following questions:

On what occasions did David pray?

What did he want from God?

How did God respond?

2. The most amazing truth seen here is that God hears and God helps and God delivers. Look at the following verses in the Psalms and write what you learn about prayer and God's response:

Psalm 4:1-3

Psalm 5:1-3

Psalm 40:1-3

Psalm 50:15

3. What is your favorite promise from your study today?

4. How will this change the way you pray to the Lord?

ADORE GOD IN PRAYER

"Thou art oft most present, Lord,
In weak distracted prayer;
A sinner out of heart with self
Most often finds Thee there.
For prayer that humbles, set the soul
From all illusions free,
And teaches it how utterly,
Dear Lord, it hangs on Thee."[4]

OSWALD CHAMBERS IN CHRISTIAN DISCIPLINES

Ask God for the following:
"For perfect childlike confidence in Thee;
For childlike glimpses of the life to be;
For trust akin to my child's trust in me;
For hearts at rest through confidence in Thee;
For hearts triumphant in perpetual hope;
For hope victorious through past hopes fulfilled;
For mightier hopes born of the things we know;
For faith born of the things we may not know;
For hope of powers increased ten thousand fold;
For that last hope of likeness to Thyself,
When hope shall end in glorious certainty;
With quickened hearts
That find Thee everywhere,
We thank Thee, Lord!"[5]

OSWALD CHAMBERS IN CHRISTIAN DISCIPLINES

YIELD YOURSELF TO GOD

Delays are not refusals; many a prayer is registered, and underneath it the words: My time is not yet come. God has a set time as well as a set purpose, and He who orders the bounds of our habitation orders also the time of our deliverance.[6]

MRS. CHARLES COWMAN IN STREAMS IN THE DESERT

If Jesus, the strong Son of God, felt it necessary to rise before the breaking of the day to pour out His heart to God in prayer, how much more ought you to pray unto Him who is the Giver of every good and perfect gift, and who has promised all things necessary for our good. What Jesus gathered into His life from His prayers we can never know, but this we do know, that the prayerless life is a powerless life. A prayerless life may be a noisy life, and fuss around a great deal; but such a life is far removed from Him who, by day and night, prayed to God.[7]

MRS. CHARLES COWMAN IN STREAMS IN THE DESERT

ENJOY HIS PRESENCE

We know from Hebrews 5:7 that Jesus "offered up both prayers and supplications with loud crying and tears to the One able to save Him from death, and He was heard because of His piety." Think about it. During His life on earth Jesus called upon His Father often and with loud crying and tears. Have you learned the secret of calling on God and pouring your heart out to Him? It is His great desire that you do exactly that. Just think, you can go into your prayer closet, wherever that quiet place may be, close the door, and step into the audience of the Creator of the Universe who is all-powerful and all-sufficient. Don't waste another second without taking advantage of your opportunity to commune with the One who holds the plan for your life in His hands. May it never be said of you or any of those who love Him, "You do not have because you do not ask" (James 4:2). Cry out today to the one who is the God of deliverances (Psalm 68:20).

REST IN HIS LOVE

"Don't worry about anything; instead, pray about everything. Tell God what you need, and thank him for all he has done. Then you will experience God's peace, which exceeds anything we can understand. His peace will guard your hearts and minds as you live in Christ Jesus" (Philippians 4:6-7 NLT).

WHAT WILL GOD DO?

He reached down from heaven and rescued me; he drew me out of deep waters.
PSALM 18:16 NLT

PREPARE YOUR HEART

Oh what a day it is when you see the rescue and the deliverance of God! Psalm 18 is such a clear picture of the passionate response of God to the cry of your heart. One thing is clear. God does not sit on the sidelines as a disinterested bystander watching the affairs of the world as so many believe. As you zoom in for a closer look at what the Lord does on David's behalf you can know that what He did for David, He can and will do for you. Ask God now to give you a willing heart and mind to believe Him to do what only He can do.

READ AND STUDY GOD'S WORD

1. Read Psalm 18 and write out everything you learn about God. There are so many wonderful and powerful truths here and it might take just a little more time than usual but oh, what treasure is to be found as you take some time to live in this most blessed destination in your current itinerary of study in the Psalms. Underline those truths that are your favorites. (For more space, you may use the next page and a journal page in the back of this book).

Truths about God in Psalm 18:

2. Write out your most important insight about God that you have learned from Psalm 18.

ADORE GOD IN PRAYER

"Our Father, sometimes Thou dost seem so far away, as if Thou art a God in hiding, as if Thou art determined to elude all who seek Thee. Yet we know that Thou art far more willing to be found than we are to seek. Thou hast promised If with all Thy heart ye truly seek me, ye shall ever surely find me. And hast Thou not assured us that Thou art with us always? Help us now to be as aware of Thy nearness as we are of the material things of every day. Help us to recognize Thy voice with as much assurance as we recognize the sounds of the world around us. We would find Thee now in the privacy of our hearts, in the quiet of this moment. We would know, our Father that Thou art near us and beside us; that Thou dost love us and art interested in all that we do, art concerned about all our affairs. May we become aware of Thy companionship, of Him who walks beside us. At times when we feel forsaken, may we know the presence of the Holy Spirit who brings comfort to all human hearts when we are willing to surrender ourselves. May we be convinced that even before we reach up to Thee, Thou art reaching down to us. These blessings, together with the unexpressed longing in our hearts, we ask in the strong name of Jesus Christ, Our Lord. Amen."[8]

PETER MARSHALL IN THE PRAYERS OF PETER MARSHALL

YIELD YOURSELF TO GOD

Meditate on the following words by Charles Haddon Spurgeon:

Dear friend, are you in trouble? Do you have a God? Then pray and spread your trial before Him. Do you have a troublesome letter in your house (2 Kin. 19:10–13)? Then go, like Hezekiah, and tell the Lord (2 Kin. 19:14). Is your child dying? Then cry to the Lord as David did (2 Sam. 12:16). Are you as low as Jonah? Then let your prayer rise from the bottom (Jon. 2:1). Are you bitter? Pour it out before the Lord. Make good use of your God. Gain full advantage by pleading with Him. Tell Him your troubles. Search His promises, and then petition Him with holy boldness, for this is the surest and the fastest way to find relief. What would we do if we could not speak with God, our ever-gracious Friend? We would die of a broken heart. Like Job, we would curse the day of our birth. We would wish that we had never been born (Job 3:3) and look forward to annihilation. But praise God, we can go to Him by faith and plead His promise. The dark clouds will withdraw, and we will come into the light and sing: This God is our God forever and ever, He will be our Guide, even unto death.[9]

Charles Haddon Spurgeon in Beside Still Waters

Enjoy His Presence

How can Spurgeon say such things about God? How can David say such things about God in Psalm 18? Because they both have firsthand experience with God. They have drawn near to Him, talked with Him, and seen Him in action in their own lives. How about you? Do you realize that God is near and ready to meet you at the heart of your own need? Tozer reminds us of a powerful truth about our God, "...God can be known in personal experience. A loving Personality dominates the Bible, walking among the trees of the garden and breathing fragrance over every scene. Always a living Person is present, speaking, pleading, loving, working, and manifesting Himself whenever and wherever His people have the receptivity necessary to receive the manifestation. The Bible assumes as a self-evident fact that men can know God with at least the same degree of immediacy as they know any other person or thing that comes within the field of their experience. The same terms are used to express the knowledge of God as are used to express knowledge of physical things. 'O taste and see that the Lord is good' (Ps. 34:8)."[10]

Will you taste and see today that God is the "God of deliverances" (Psalm 68:20)? Close by writing a prayer to the Lord expressing all that is on your heart.

Rest in His Love

"God is to us a God of deliverances; and to God the Lord belong escapes from death" (Psalm 68:20).

WHAT WILL I LEARN ABOUT GOD?

For who is God, but the LORD? And who is a rock, except our God…He makes my feet like hinds feet, and sets me upon my high places…You have given me the shield of Your salvation, and Your right hand upholds me; and Your gentleness makes me great.
PSALM 18:31, 33, 35 NLT

PREPARE YOUR HEART

There is a stance utterly peculiar to the world and standard for the Christian who knows who God is and what He does. That stance is praise in advance. Spurgeon says, "Though you have no income to meet your needs and are brought to poverty's door, nonetheless, bless the Lord. His mighty providence cannot fail so long as one of His children needs to be provided for. Your song, while you are in distress, will be sweet music to God's ear. Go in the name of God. Meet your difficulties calmly and fairly. Do not have any plans or tricks, just commit yourself to God. This is the way you may confidently find deliverance. If you can only trust and praise God, you will see marvelous things that will utterly astonish you."[11]

You may be thinking, "How can I possibly do this? What if He doesn't come through? What if I never hear from God again?" Today you will look at what David learned about God's character and work. You can know this: all that God did for David He can do for you. His plan for you may be different than His plan for David. However, God is still the same God "who is able to do immeasurably more than all we ask or imagine, according to the power that is at work within us" (Ephesians 3:20). And God does have a plan for you that offers a future and a hope (Jeremiah 29:11). Ask God now to speak to your heart and show you who He is and what He wants to teach you about Himself.

READ AND STUDY GOD'S WORD

1. David learned some amazing truths about God as a result of his experience with Him. Read the following verses and underline those that are most significant to you today:

"For You light my lamp:
The LORD my God illumines my darkness.

For by You I can run upon a troop;
And by my God I can leap over a wall.
As for God, His way is blameless;
The word of the LORD is tried;
He is a shield to all who take refuge in Him.
For who is God, but the LORD?
And who is a rock, except our God,
The God who girds me with strength
And makes my way blameless?
He makes my feet like hinds feet,
And sets me upon my high places.
He trains my hands for battle,
So that my arms can bend a bow of bronze.
You have also given me the shield of Your salvation,
And Your right hand upholds me;
And Your gentleness makes me great.
You enlarge my steps under me,
And my feet have not slipped."

PSALM 18:28-36

2. David learned so much about God. He saw God at work in a powerful way in his own life. What is most significant to you about what God did in David's life? Why does it mean so much to you?

ADORE GOD IN PRAYER

Turn to your prayer pages in the back of this book and use one of the pages for you and your needs. Record all the requests that are on your heart, one by one in the spaces provided. Then, watch eagerly in the days to come as God responds to your prayers.

YIELD YOURSELF TO GOD

Meditate on these choice thoughts from Charles Haddon Spurgeon in *The Treasury Of David*:

For You light my lamp; The LORD my God illumines my darkness—the presence of the Lord removes all the gloom of sorrow, and enables the believer to rejoice with exceeding great joy. The lighting of the lamp is a cheerful moment in the winter's evening, but the lifting up of the light of God's countenance is happier far (more). It is said that the poor in Egypt will stint themselves of bread to buy oil for the lamp, so that they may not sit in darkness; we could well afford to part with all earthly comforts if the light of God's love could but constantly gladden our souls.

The word of the Lord is tried—The doctrines are glorious, the precepts are pure, the promises are faithful, and the whole revelation is superlatively full of grace and truth. David had tried it, thousands have tried it, we have tried it, and it has never failed.

For who is God, but the LORD? And who is a rock, except our God—Where can lasting hopes be fixed? Where can the soul find rest? Where is stability to be found? Where is strength to be discovered? Surely in the Lord Jehovah alone can we find rest and refuge.

He makes my feet like hinds feet, and sets me upon my high places—Pursuing his foes the warrior had been swift of foot as a young roe, but instead of taking pleasure in the legs of a man, he ascribes the boon of swiftness to the Lord alone. When our thoughts are nimble, and our spirits rapid, like the chariots of Amminadib, let us not forget that our best Beloved's hand has given us the choice favour. Climbing into impregnable fortresses, David had been preserved from slipping, and made to stand where scarce the wild goat can find a footing; herein was preserving mercy manifested.

Your gentleness makes me great—David saw much of benevolence in God's action towards him, and he gratefully ascribed all his greatness not to his own goodness, but to the goodness of God…It is God making himself little which is the cause of our being made great. We are so little that if God should manifest his greatness without condescension, we should be trampled under his feet; but God, who must stoop to view the skies and bow to see what angels do, looks to the lowly and contrite, and makes them great…David ascribes all his own greatness to the condescending goodness and graciousness of his Father in heaven. Let us all feel this sentiment in our own hearts, and confess that whatever of goodness or greatness God may have put upon us, we must cast our crowns at his feet, and cry *thy gentleness hath made me great.*[12]

CHARLES HADDON SPURGEON IN THE TREASURY OF DAVID

ENJOY HIS PRESENCE

Some, out of great despair and discouragement, have accused and blamed God, hoping to arouse God's interest and action. David never blamed God but he did have a time of despair as can be seen in his words in Psalm 13:1, "How long, O LORD? Will you forget me forever?" Psalm 18 gives the other side of the trial and what David learned about God and His ways when God delivered him. Here's your challenge—will you launch out in faith and see God in your trial and realize that the God that David knew is your God as well? Will you taste and see that the LORD is good (Psalm 34:8). May He illumine your darkness, may His right hand uphold you, and may His gentleness make you great. God bless you today, dear friend.

REST IN HIS LOVE

"Though the fig tree should not blossom and there be no fruit on the vines, though the yield of the olive should fail and the fields produce no food, though the flock should be cut off from the fold and there be no cattle in the stalls, yet I will exult in the LORD, I will rejoice in the God of my salvation. The Lord God is my strength, and He has made my feet like hinds feet, and makes me walk on my high places" (Habakkuk 3:17-19).

WHAT WILL I DO?

For this, O LORD, I will praise you among the nations; I will sing praises to your name.
PSALM 18:49 NLT

PREPARE YOUR HEART

One dark day, during her quiet time, Darlene Zschech sat down at her old, out of tune piano. She was so discouraged and desperate for peace that she opened her Bible to the Psalms. She began playing and thus was borne one of the most heartfelt popular worship songs ever written, Shout To The Lord. She sang the song over and over again in her time of despair and found that this song of praise that had come to her lifted her from despair to faith in God. Shout To The Lord is a song of praise and worship that has come out of time of great despair. Since that time it has been recorded on more than twenty albums and sung worldwide by thousands and thousands of people. One song of praise can so lift the heart and the spirit that it can change a life forever. Worship and praise is a choice and oh, how precious it is to your Lord especially when you feel discouraged. It is one of those extraordinary actions that those who walk by faith learn in the crucible of great suffering.

Begin your quiet time with the Lord by reading or singing this hymn, *Praise To The Lord, The Almighty*, written by Joachim Neander:

> Praise to the Lord, the Almighty, the King of creation!
>
> O my soul, praise Him, for He is thy health and salvation!
>
> All ye who hear, Now to His temple draw near;
>
> Join me in glad adoration!
>
>
> Praise to the Lord, who o'er all things so wondrously reigneth,
>
> Shelters thee under His wings, yes, so gently sustaineth!
>
> Hast thou not seen how all thy longings have been
>
> Granted in what He ordaineth?

Praise to the Lord, who doth prosper thy work and defend thee;

Surely His goodness and mercy here daily attend thee.

Ponder anew what the Almighty can do,

If with His love He befriend thee.

Praise to the Lord! O let all that is in me adore Him!

All that hath life and breath, come now with praises before Him.

Let the amen sound from His people again;

Gladly for aye we adore Him. Amen.

READ AND STUDY GOD'S WORD

1. This is our last day in Psalm 18. It always seems sad to leave one area of Scripture but there is joy ahead as we have more landscape to traverse in the Psalms. Today we want to look at David's conclusion to all that God has done in his life. Read Psalm 18:49-50 and write what David has resolved to do in response to God's deliverance.

2. Thanksgiving and praise to God is taught throughout the Bible and is seen in the lives of the great men and women who have known and loved God. Look at the following verses and record what you learn.

Ephesians 5:18-20

Philippians 4:6-7

Colossians 3:15-17

1 Thessalonians 5:18

Hebrews 13:15

3. Why is it difficult in a time of discouragement to praise the Lord and what is it that enables a child of God to have a heart of praise?

4. What have you learned that will help you to offer a heart of gratitude in your own trials?

ADORE GOD IN PRAYER

Will you take some time now to offer thanksgiving to the Lord? Think of four things in your life that you are thankful for. They may be simple or more detailed praises. But give the Lord a heart of worship today, thanking and praising Him. Write out your greatest praise and carry it with you throughout the day.

YIELD YOURSELF TO GOD

"Sing a new song to the LORD! Let the whole earth sing to the LORD!
Sing to the LORD; praise his name. Each day proclaim the good news that he
saves.

Publish his glorious deeds among the nations. Tell everyone about the amazing things he does.

Great is the LORD! He is most worthy of praise! He is to be feared above all gods.

The gods of other nations are mere idols, but the LORD made the heavens!

Honor and majesty surround him; strength and beauty fill his sanctuary.

O nations of the world, recognize the LORD; recognize that the LORD is glorious and strong.

Give to the LORD the glory he deserves! Bring your offerings and come into his courts.

Worship the LORD in all his holy splendor. Let all the earth tremble before him.

Tell all the nations, The LORD reigns! The world stands firm and cannot be shaken.

He will judge all peoples fairly.

Let the heavens be glad, and the earth rejoice! Let the sea and everything in it shout his praise!

Let the fields and their crops burst out with joy! Let the trees of the forest rustle with praise before the Lord, for he is coming! He is coming to judge the earth. He will judge the world with justice, and the nations with his truth."

PSALM 96 NLT

ENJOY HIS PRESENCE

David, the man after God's own heart, demonstrated extraordinary, even extravagant worship of His Lord. He is described in 2 Samuel 6:14 as "dancing before the Lord with all his might." Can you just see him praising the Lord. Today, as you go about your day, think often about the example of David and all you have learned from his psalm. Then, praise and worship God.

REST IN HIS LOVE

"Through Him then, let us continually offer up a sacrifice of praise to God, that is, the fruit of lips that give thanks to His name" (Hebrews 13:15).

DEVOTIONAL READING
BY JAMES MONTGOMERY BOICE

DEAR FRIEND,

This week you looked at how to have hope when you are discouraged. Look back over your week of study and summarize what you learned from David in Psalm 18.

What were your most meaningful discoveries this week as you spent time with the Lord?

Most meaningful insight:

Most meaningful devotional reading:

Most meaningful verse:

The dominant theme of Psalm 18 is that God is our Rock!...this means he is a shelter beside which we can be protected and prosper, a fortress into which we can run and be safe, a firm foundation upon which our shaking feet can stand and upon which we can build. But I remember also the way in which the great eighteenth-century preacher and songwriter Augustus M. Toplady (1740-1778) handled it in Rock of Ages. Toplady was traveling in the country when a storm came upon him and he was forced to take shelter in the cleft of a great rock. While he was waiting for the storm to pass he reflected on the situation spiritually, and the words of a hymn began to form in his mind…

Rock of Ages, cleft for me,

Let me hide myself in thee;

Let the water and the blood,

From thy wounded side which flowed,

Be of sin the double cure,

Cleanse me from its guilt and power.

Rock of Ages, cleft for me,

Let me hide myself in thee.[13]

JAMES MONTGOMERY BOICE IN PSALMS VOLUME 1

Viewer Guide

❧ WEEK FOUR ☙

The Rescue Of The Lord

In Week Four of *A Heart That Hopes In God*, you had the opportunity to study Psalm 18, one of the most exciting rescues by God recorded in the Bible. In this case, David, the man after God's own heart, is the one being rescued. And oh, what a rescue it was! So, grab your Bibles, and let's talk about this magnificent rescue by God.

"He sent from on high, He took me; He drew me out of many waters" (Psalm 18:16).

Some Observations about God in Psalm 18

1. God has great _____for those He loves. Psalm 18:19

The word for "delight" is *chaphets* and means *to have an affection for*.

2. In this psalm we see the _____of our God. Psalm 18:7, 10

3. In this psalm we see the _____nature of our God. Psalm 18:16

4. God will _____you. Psalm 18:19

The word "rescue" is *chalats* and means *to deliver, draw out, extricate*.

In God's rescue, He _____you. Isaiah 41:10

In God's rescue, He _____you. 2 Corinthians 1:3

In God's rescue, He _____ you.
Isaiah 41:4

In God's rescue, He _____ you.
Psalm 119:176

In God's rescue, He _____ you.
2 Corinthians 3:18

In God's rescue, He _____ you.
Psalm 18:6

In God's rescue, He _____ you.
Psalm 86:7

"Not one of the good promises which the LORD had made to the house of Israel failed; all came to pass" (Joshua 21:45).

Video messages are available on DVDs or as Downloadable M4V Video. Audio messages are available on Audio CDs or as Downloadable MP3 Audio. Visit the Quiet Time Ministries Online Store at www.quiettime.org.

HOPE WHEN YOU NEED DELIVERANCE

Psalm 34

Hope fills the afflicted soul with such inward joy and consolation, that it can laugh while tears are in the eye, sigh and sing all in a breath; it is called "The rejoicing of hope" (Hebrews 13:6).

WILLIAM GURNALL

THE GOD OF DELIVERANCES

I sought the LORD, and He answered me, and delivered me from all my fears.
PSALM 34:4

PREPARE YOUR HEART

What difference does it really make that the Lord is in your life? That is what the world wants to know. And the enemy of your soul would have you believe that there is no difference at all. In fact, at times, in the face of trials and companion fears, there are thoughts that perhaps God is not going to come through after all.

When you read through the Old Testament, you see again and again that the enemies of God challenged the people of Israel with the lie that their God could not and would not save them. Hezekiah is a perfect example (2 Kings 18). Sennacherib, king of Assyria, blatantly defied God and told Hezekiah in a letter that God was deceiving him, would never deliver the people, and would be defeated by the people of Assyria (2 Kings 19:10). Those words sounded convincing. And the lie of the enemy often seems more true in the heat of the trial. Hezekiah spread that threatening letter from Sennacherib out before the Lord and cried out to God: "Now, O LORD our God, I pray, deliver us from his hand that all the kingdoms of the earth may know that You alone, O LORD, are God" (2 Kings 19:14-19). What happened? God answered Hezekiah through Isaiah, "Thus says the LORD, the God of Israel, 'Because you have prayed to Me about Sennacherib king of Assyria, I have heard you'" (2 Kings 19:20). Ultimately, the Lord delivered His people. He killed 185,000 Assyrians while they were sleeping. The people of Israel did not even need to fight the battle. Sennacharib was killed by his own people.

Consider the case of Nehemiah, appointed by God to rebuild the walls of Jerusalem following the Babylonian captivity (Nehemiah 6). The enemies of God rose up against Nehemiah many times falsely accusing him of rebellion in the hopes that he would become afraid and stop rebuilding the wall. Nehemiah 6:9 reveals that Nehemiah knew exactly what the enemy was trying to do: "For all of them were trying to frighten us, thinking, 'They will become discouraged with the work and it will not be done.'" What did Nehemiah do? He cried out to His God, "But now, O God, strengthen my hands" (Nehemiah 6:9). And what did God do? He enabled Nehemiah and the people to complete the work (Nehemiah 6:15). And what about those threatening enemies who were so convincing with their cutting words? Nehemiah gives the rest of the story: "When all our enemies heard of it (the completed wall), and all the nations surrounding us saw it, they lost their confidence; for they recognized that this work had been accomplished with the help of our God" (Nehemiah 6:16).

This week you are going to have the privilege to step onto the holy ground of Psalm 34, a psalm all about deliverance. You need deliverance every day of your life and the good news is that God is the God of deliverances—"God is to us a God of deliverances; and to God the LORD belong escapes from death" (Psalm 68:20). Deliverance means rescue and salvation. It means that you are moved from a place of distress to the wide space of safety and security. It means that somehow, in some way, God is going to work in you and in your circumstances. He is the God of deliverances. Draw near to God now, and ask Him to speak to you in His Word.

READ AND STUDY GOD'S WORD

1. Begin your time in God's Word today by turning to Psalm 68:20. Write this verse out word-for-word in the space provided. Then, underline the words "deliverances" and "escapes" to focus on the powerful truth of this verse.

2. Psalm 34 was written by David as a result of a great deliverance in the midst of his trial with King Saul. Imagine being chased by the most powerful man in the world. You have seen this before in other psalms. However, David's trial was most heated when he realized from Saul's son, Jonathan, that Saul really did intend to kill him. He was forced to run for his life. He ran to Achish king of Gath (also known as Abimelech in Psalm 34), hoping for help. But he quickly realized that Achish would betray him and so David feigned insanity and was able to escape. As you begin your time in Psalm 34, read the background of the psalm in 1 Samuel 21:10-22:1. How do you think David felt at this time in his life?

3. Read Psalm 34 slowly and carefully. What title would you give this psalm?

4. What is your favorite verse in Psalm 34 today and why?

ADORE GOD IN PRAYER

As you think about what you read in Psalm 34, do you have any fears you are facing? If so, will you take those fears to the Lord today? Spread them out before the Lord like Hezekiah (2 Kings 19:14-19). Ask Him to deliver you from all your fears (Psalm 34:4).

YIELD YOURSELF TO GOD

> David's circumstances did not immediately change. He was still a fugitive. He was still in danger. For a time at least he was still alone. But God did deliver him from Achish; that is, he preserved his life. And his grim circumstances did begin to change. The future leaders of his kingdom began to come to him. That is important. The promise of prayer does not mean that God will change every difficult thing in your life. But he will preserve you for as long as he has work for you to do, and he will transform even the difficult circumstances by his presence and perhaps the presence of others whom he sends to be with you.[1]
>
> JAMES MONTGOMERY BOICE IN PSALMS VOLUME 1

Are you in great trouble? If you have a trial that you cannot share or a trouble that, if you did share, no one could help, then go and spread it before the Lord. Remember His words, "Many are the afflictions of the righteous, but the LORD delivers him out of them all" (Ps. 34:19). Go and tell Him that He has spoken and that He has pledged Himself to deliver you out of all your afflictions. Be sure of this, God will be as good as His Word. My brothers and sisters, may God help us to look to Him.[2]

CHARLES HADDON SPURGEON IN BESIDE STILL WATERS

ENJOY HIS PRESENCE

Today is your day to realize that God is a "God of deliverances." Note that the word "deliverances" is plural. Isn't it wonderful to know that nothing can come your way that is too great for Him to handle. He is the one who holds the key to everything you are facing today. You can know this—He has delivered (rescued and saved) His people thousands of times in the past and He will continue to deliver until all His children are in their eternal home with Him forever. Why? Because it is in His very nature and Person to deliver His people. He is the God of deliverances. He stands near, ready to rescue when you are in trouble. He sees when no one sees and He will help when no one helps. His deliverances come in many ways—there is deliverance out of a circumstance and sometimes, like David experienced while being chased by Saul, there is deliverance in and through the circumstance. So, dear friend, be strong and courageous today and know that in His time and in His way, the God of deliverances will rescue, help, answer and save you. Close by writing a prayer to the Lord thanking Him for who He is and what He does.

REST IN HIS LOVE

"Blessed be the LORD, my rock, who trains my hands for war, and my fingers for battle; my lovingkindness and my fortress, my stronghold and my deliverer, my shield and He in whom I take refuge..." (Psalm 144:1-2).

THOSE WHO CRY OUT

This poor man cried, and the LORD heard him, and saved him out of all his troubles.
PSALM 34:6

PREPARE YOUR HEART

Years ago a poor woman, accompanied by two of her neighbors, came to Charles Spurgeon's office in deep distress. Her husband had fled the country; in her sorrow she came to church, and something he said in his sermon led her to believe he knew about her situation. Of course, Spurgeon knew nothing about her. The illustration he used just happened to meet her in her own sad circumstance. She told him her story and Spurgeon said, "There is nothing that we can do but to kneel down and cry to the Lord for the immediate conversion of your husband." They knelt down, and Spurgeon prayed that the Lord would touch the heart of the deserter, convert his soul and bring him back to his home. When they rose from their knees he said to this poor woman, "Do not fret about the matter. I feel sure your husband will come home; and that he will yet become connected with our church." She left his office, and Spurgeon forgot all about it.

Some months later, she reappeared with her neighbors and a man, whom she introduced to Spurgeon as her husband. He had indeed returned home, and he had come to know Christ. On the very day that Spurgeon and the woman had prayed for his conversion, he was on a ship far away on the sea. That very day he stumbled most unexpectedly upon a stray copy of one of Spurgeon's sermons. He read it and the truth convicted his heart. He repented and sought the Lord, and as soon as possible he returned to his wife and to his daily calling. He became a member of Spurgeon's church. All the skeptics in the world could never shake that woman's conviction and personal experience that there is a God who hears her cries and answers. Spurgeon said of the experience, "I do not regard it as miraculous; it is part and parcel of the established order of the universe that the shadow of the coming event should fall in advance upon some believing soul in the shape of prayer for its realization. The prayer of faith is a divine decree commencing its fulfillment."[3]

Who cries out to the Lord? It is one like that woman who realized her own need and placed her dependence on her all-sufficient all-powerful God, the One who was greater than herself. When David spoke of his experience, he said "This poor man cried, and the Lord heard him, and saved him out of all his troubles" (Psalm 34:6). It is those who are "poor" who cry out and the Lord hears and saves. What does it mean to be "poor?" That's what we will look at today. Come near to the Lord now and lay your heart before Him and ask Him to speak to you. What are the needs pressing in on you today? Write a short prayer to Him, giving Him what is on your heart.

READ AND STUDY GOD'S WORD

1. Read Psalm 34:6 and write it out, word-for-word.

2. It is those who are "poor" who will cry out and who are heard by the Lord. What does it mean to be "poor" in the sense that it is used by David? The word in the Hebrew is *ani* and means one who is weak, humble, afflicted and in distress. It is a person who is distressed or may be experiencing a disability of some kind. The distress is such that the person is utterly defenseless. Only when you realize you are "poor" will you cry out to God and place your hope in Him. And when you step back and think about it, is not every believer in a position of need before the God of the Universe? Who can take a breath without God? Everything we have is from the Lord. Man is only deluded to think that he has any power without his sovereign God. Here is what God had to say to the people of Israel when they began to forget about Him in their lives: "Woe to those who go down to Egypt for help and rely on horses, and trust in chariots because they are many and in horsemen because they are very strong, but they do not look to the Holy One of Israel, nor seek the LORD!" (Isaiah 31:1). We must always be in the position of looking to the Lord to meet our every need. What is required to get to that place in your relationship with God? Humility. The humble person realizes his place before the all-powerful, all-sufficient God. Alan Redpath has said, "The best place any Christian can ever be in is to be totally destitute and totally dependant upon God, and know it." Peter offers some encouragement in this regard. Read the following verses and underline those phrases that are most important to you today:

"'God opposes the proud but favors the humble.' So humble yourselves under the mighty power of God, and at the right time he will lift you up in honor. Give all your worries and cares to God, for he cares about you" (1 Peter 5:6-7 NLT).

"In his kindness God called you to share in his eternal glory by means of Christ Jesus. So after you have suffered a little while, he will restore, support, and strengthen you, and he will place you on a firm foundation. All power to him forever! Amen" (1 Peter 5:10-11 NLT).

3. Sometimes it is the suffering that takes us to the place of humility so that we will look to the Lord at every turn in our life. But when the people of God cry out, God delivers—it is out of His very nature that, at the cry of His children, He listens and saves. Look at the following verses and record what you learn about crying out to God:

Judges 3:9, 15

2 Kings 13:4-5

Nehemiah 9:27-28

Isaiah 41:17-20

ADORE GOD IN PRAYER

Have you cried out to the Lord daily about every need in your life? The Lord hears your cries and out of His heart of compassion as the God of deliverances, He will meet your deepest need from His vast resources in ways you cannot even imagine. That is what He does. He is the God who loves to bring springs in the midst of a valley. Cry out to Him today with every single need on your heart. You may even want to turn to your prayer pages and devote one page to the needs in your life. Be sure to mark the date so you can watch God abundantly answer your prayer.

YIELD YOURSELF TO GOD

This is a psalm for *poor* men—and poor women too. It is a psalm for all who are alone or destitute—for you, if you have nothing at all or are not even sure that you will live long. It is for people who find themselves at the absolute low point in life, which is where David was. Or find themselves between a rock, which in this case was King Saul, and a hard place, which was King Achish. It is for you when everything seems against you.[4]

JAMES MONTGOMERY BOICE IN PSALMS VOLUME 1

God's greatest movements in this world have been conditioned on, continued and fashioned by prayer. God has put Himself in these great movements just as men have prayed. Persistent, prevailing, conspicuous and mastering prayer has always brought God to be present. How vast are the possibilities of prayer! How wide its reach! It lays its hand on Almighty God and moves Him to do what He would not do if prayer was not offered. Prayer is a wonderful power placed by Almighty God in the hands of His saints, which may be used to accomplish great purposes and to achieve unusual results. The only limits to prayer are the promises of God and His ability to fulfill those promises.[5]

E.M. BOUNDS IN THE POSSIBILITIES OF PRAYER

ENJOY HIS PRESENCE

The greatest deliverance God has accomplished is the rescue by Jesus of those doomed to eternal death because of sin. His death on the cross and resurrection was God's response to the cry of the suffering human race (Isaiah 53, Romans 11:26-27). If the Lord has accomplished such a great deliverance through Christ, then surely He will respond to your need. John Henry Jowett says, "Our best asking always falls immeasurably short of the Father's giving."[6] Thank the Lord today for hearing your cries with the knowledge that He hears and He will answer you and deliver you.

REST IN HIS LOVE

"The afflicted and needy are seeking water, but there is none, and their tongue is parched with thirst; I, the LORD, will answer them myself, As the God of Israel I will not forsake them" (Isaiah 41:17).

THOSE WHO TASTE AND SEE

O taste and see that the LORD is good; how blessed is the man who takes refuge in Him.
PSALM 34:8

PREPARE YOUR HEART

We have been looking at what happens when you are in need of a rescue. That's what the need for deliverance is all about—hemmed in on every side and no way out. We have learned that there is One greater than ourselves, our Lord who is the God of deliverances. How can we know His deliverance, His rescue in our own lives? Cry out to the Lord. David is our great example as one who was in a position of need, and from that place he humbled himself and cried out to his great God.

In this psalm, David issues forth one of the great invitations found in the Bible: "O taste and see that the LORD is good" (Psalm 34:8). These words are the product of his very real experience with God. Here's what makes these words so powerful. It is one thing to encourage others to taste and see that the Lord is good when the sun is shining brightly but quite another in the darkness of a desperate trial. And herein is the secret for you to make it through your desperate hour. Sit at the banquet table of the Lord. The result is magnificent blessing.

Meditate on the following words by Robert Robinson (1735-1790) as you draw near to the God in your quiet time today. You might even sing it to the Lord if you know the melody.

> Come, thou Fount of every blessing,
>
> tune my heart to sing thy grace;
>
> streams of mercy, never ceasing,
>
> call for songs of loudest praise.
>
> Teach me some melodious sonnet,
>
> sung by flaming tongues above.
>
> Praise the mount! I'm fixed upon it,
>
> mount of thy redeeming love.

Here I raise mine Ebenezer; (1 Samuel 7:12 Ebenezer means "the stone of help")

hither by thy help I'm come;

and I hope, by thy good pleasure,

safely to arrive at home.

Jesus sought me when a stranger,

wandering from the fold of God;

He, to rescue me from danger,

interposed His precious blood.

O to grace how great a debtor

daily I'm constrained to be!

Let thy goodness, like a fetter,

bind my wandering heart to thee.

Prone to wander, Lord, I feel it,

prone to leave the God I love;

here's my heart, O take and seal it,

seal it for thy courts above.

READ AND STUDY GOD'S WORD

1. What does it mean to taste and see that the Lord is good? It is an encouragement to "try God out" as we would some rare delicacy and when we do, we will see that He is good, pleasant, beautiful, excellent, lovely, delightful, convenient, joyful, fruitful, precious, sound, cheerful, kind, correct, and righteous.[7]

Look at the following verses and write what you learn that will help you understand what it means to "taste and see that the Lord is good." Include in your insights and observations what you "see" about the Lord in these verses.

1 Chronicles 29:11-12

Psalm 46:10

Jeremiah 9:23-24

Jeremiah 15:15-16

Lamentations 3:19-25

2. Describe in your own words what it means to "taste and see that the Lord is good"?

3. What benefits do you think a person will experience if they "taste and see that the Lord is good" in the midst of time of distress and desperation?

4. As you run to the Lord and make Him your refuge, Psalm 34:8 says "how blessed" you are. In this case, "blessed" means happiness or bliss. Imagine such a state in the midst of trouble. This experience of bliss or happiness is a rescue of another kind and one that sets the Christian apart

from those in the world. The word "blessed" is seen in the beatitudes (Matthew 5:3-11) and is *makarios* in the Greek. The "blessed" person is "one whom God makes fully satisfied, not because of favorable circumstances, but because He indwells the believer through Christ…*Makarios* is the one who is in the world yet independent of the world, his satisfaction comes from God and not from favorable circumstances."[8]

ADORE GOD IN PRAYER

What is the one prayer on your heart today? Turn to your prayer pages and write out your request and talk with the Lord about it.

YIELD YOURSELF TO GOD

How does God become a part of you, a part of your thinking, of what you really are? It is by faith, and faith means believing God and acting upon that belief. In other words, it is exactly what David is speaking of in this stanza, though in other words. He wants us to act on what we know of God and his goodness, for only then will we actually experience for ourselves how good God truly is.[9]

JAMES MONTGOMERY BOICE IN PSALMS VOLUME 1

ENJOY HIS PRESENCE

Will you take time to "taste and see that the Lord is good" at the feast of His banquet table today? When you do, you will be blessed. Close by writing a prayer expressing all that is on your heart to the Lord.

REST IN HIS LOVE

"Be still, and know that I am God" (Psalm 46:10 NLT).

THOSE WHO SEEK THE LORD

The young lions do lack and suffer hunger; but they who seek
the LORD shall not be in want of any good thing.
PSALM 34:10

PREPARE YOUR HEART

Sometimes in the heart of a passage of Scripture a verse sparkles with the light of a promise. Psalm 34:10 is just such a jewel, boldly promising that "they who seek the LORD shall not be in want of any good thing." Meditate on this diamond of a verse in these different translations as a preparation of heart today.

"The young lions lack food and suffer hunger, but they who seek [inquire of and require] the Lord [by right of their need and on the authority of His Word], none of them shall lack any beneficial thing." AMP

"Even strong young lions sometimes go hungry, but those who trust in the LORD will never lack any good thing." NLT

"Even lions may get weak and hungry, but those who look to the Lord will have every good thing." NCV

READ AND STUDY GOD'S WORD

1. When you look at a diamond it is the clarity and the way it is cut that sends forth a certain sparkle. And so it is with Scripture. The clarity of it is more apparent the longer you look at it. The facets of Scripture are infinite. Look at the following verses and record what you learn about the Lord. Personalize your observations i.e. "The Lord will provide for me…"

Genesis 22:14 This is the name of God, Yahweh Jireh meaning "The Lord sees and provides"

Deuteronomy 33:26-29

Psalm 84:11-12

Philippians 4:19

2. To "seek the Lord" means to pursue the Lord, search Him out, and investigate Him with great care and concern. God promises in Jeremiah 29:13, "You will seek Me and find Me when you search for Me with all your heart." What have you learned today that you will "find" in God, when you seek Him?

3. Oh how wonderful it is to know that the Lord supplies your needs. He promises to give you every "good" thing. If it's good, you'll have it. And if it's not, of course, you don't want it. In the trial, God gives you the gift of Himself and He is enough for every circumstance. What is your favorite insight from your time with God in His Word today?

ADORE GOD IN PRAYER

I prayed for strength, and then I lost awhile
All sense of nearness, human and divine;
The love I leaned on failed and pierced my heart;
The hands I clung to loosed themselves from mine;
But while I swayed, weak, trembling, and alone,
The everlasting arms upheld my own.

I prayed for light; the sun went down in clouds,
The moon was darkened by a misty doubt,
The stars of heaven were dimmed by earthly fears,
And all my little candle flames burned out;
But while I sat in shadow, wrapped in night,
The face of Christ made all the darkness bright.

I prayed for peace, and dreamed of restful ease,
A slumber drugged from pain, a hushed repose;
Above my head the skies were black with storm,
And fiercer grew the onslaught of my foes;
But while the battle raged, and wild winds blew,
I heard His voice, and perfect peace I knew.

I thank Thee, Lord, Thou wert too wise to heed
My feeble prayers, and answer as I sought,
Since these rich gifts Thy bounty has bestowed
Have brought me more than I had asked or thought.
Giver of good, so answer each request
With Thine own giving, better than my best.[10]

ANNIE JOHNSON FLINT IN BEST-LOVED POEMS

YIELD YOURSELF TO GOD

Are you in doubt? One voice may say to you, 'Come this way.' Prudence may suggest to you one thing, faith another. Worldly wisdom says this path, but the voice of the Spirit says that path. If you are not sure, get alone somewhere with God until every other voice is silent and all human opinions are shut out, and learn to look to the Lord.[11]

ALAN REDPATH IN THE MAKING OF A MAN OF GOD

To trust God is better policy than the craftiest politicians can teach or practise… No really good thing shall be denied to those whose first and main end in life is to seek the Lord. Men may call them fools, but the Lord will prove them wise. They shall win where the world's wiseacres lose their all, and God shall have the glory of it.[12]

CHARLES HADDON SPURGEON IN THE TREASURY OF DAVID VOLUME I

ENJOY HIS PRESENCE

How can you apply this promise to your life today? What will be necessary in your own life to seek and trust the Lord? Rest in the promise that "those who trust in the LORD will lack no good thing" (Psalm 34:10 NLT).

REST IN HIS LOVE

"For the LORD God is a sun and shield; The LORD gives grace and glory; No good thing does He withhold from those who walk uprightly. O LORD of hosts, how blessed is the man who trusts in You" (Psalm 84:11-12).

THOSE WHO ARE RIGHTEOUS

The righteous cry, and the LORD hears, and delivers them out of all their troubles.
Psalm 34:17

Prepare Your Heart

In Psalm 34 David speaks of something that applies only to a special group of people on earth—those who know the Lord through a personal relationship with Him. He speaks of the privileges of the righteous. Oh how powerful these truths are for those who need hope in the midst of a desperate situation. Today you will learn what it means to be "righteous" and the great privileges that are yours as a result.

In preparation for your time with the Lord, think about the words of this hymn by John Newton:

Amazing grace! how sweet the sound

That saved a wretch like me!

I once was lost, but now am found,

Was blind, but now I see.

'Twas grace that taught my heart to fear,

And grace my fears relieved;

How precious did that grace appear

The hour I first believed!

When we've been there ten thousand years,

Bright shining as the sun,

We've no less days to sing God's praise

Than when we've first begun.

READ AND STUDY GOD'S WORD

1. Read Psalm 34:15-22 and write everything you learn about the righteous.

2. What does it mean to be righteous? That word is *dikaios* in the Greek and means right standing before God. It means that we perfectly meet the righteous, just standard of God. The question is, "how can that be?" when we know according to Romans 3:10 that "there is none righteous, not even one" and according to Romans 3:23 "all have sinned and fall short of the glory of God." When you receive Christ as your Savior and surrender your life to Him you are declared and made righteous by a means outside yourself—it is by Jesus' death on the cross.

Read Romans 5:17-21 and you can see these powerful truths for yourself: "For if by the transgression of the one, death reigned through the one, much more those who receive the abundance of grace and of the gift of righteousness will reign in life through the One, Jesus Christ. So then as through one transgression there resulted condemnation to all men, even so through one act of righteousness there resulted justification of life to all men. For as through the one man's disobedience the many were made sinners, even so through the obedience of the One the many will be made righteous."

Describe in your own words what Christ has done for you.

3. Think about the great privileges seen in Psalm 34 that are granted to you as one of the righteous and describe each privilege (Personalize your insights i.e. "the Lord sees and hears my cry):

"The eyes of the LORD are toward the righteous and His ears are open to their cry" (verse 15)

The privilege:

"The righteous cry, and the LORD hears and delivers them out of all their troubles" (verse 17)
The privilege:

"The LORD is near to the brokenhearted and saves those who are crushed in spirit" (verse 18)
The privilege:

"Many are the afflictions (misery, distress) of the righteous, but the LORD delivers him out of them all" (verse 19)
The privilege:

"Evil shall slay the wicked, and those who hate the righteous will be condemned" (verse 21)
The privilege:

"The LORD redeems the soul of His servants, and none of those who take refuge in Him will be condemned." (verse 22)
The privilege:

ADORE GOD IN PRAYER

Pray the words of F.B. Meyer today: "Lord Jesus! Teach me how to apply to the common things of daily life the heavenly principles of the risen life. May I think of nothing as common or unclean. May every common bush be aflame with God."[13]

YIELD YOURSELF TO GOD

The Father, in the Son, has stooped to the very lowest point of man's moral condition, that, by stooping, He might raise man to the very highest point of blessedness, in fellowship with Himself. From all this, it follows that our sonship, with all its consequent dignities and privileges, is entirely independent of us. We have just as little to do with it as Abraham's dead body and Sarah's dead womb had to do with a seed as numerous as the stars which garnish the heavens, or as the sand on the sea-shore. It is all of the Father. God the Father drew the plan, God the Son laid the foundation, and God the Holy Spirit raises the superstructure; and on this superstructure appears the inscription: "Through grace, by faith, without works of the law.[14]

C.H. MACKINTOSH

ENJOY HIS PRESENCE

Do you see that when you established a relationship with Christ by surrendering your life to Him you were made righteous? Your sins are forgiven and you have been given eternal life. And now you have the privileges of the righteous including prayer and intimacy with God. He is near to you and promises to save you when you are crushed in spirit. What that means for you is that when you are in what many have called the dark night of the soul, you are never alone. He is with you. As Paul said, "What shall we say about such wonderful things as these? If God is for us, who can ever be against us?" (Romans 8:31 NLT). Close by thinking about these words from Jeremiah: "But the LORD stands beside me like a great warrior. Before him my persecutors will stumble. They cannot defeat me. They will fail and be thoroughly humiliated. Their dishonor will never be forgotten…Sing to the LORD! Praise the LORD! For though I was poor and needy, he rescued me from my oppressors" (Jeremiah 20:11, 13).

REST IN HIS LOVE

"The name of the LORD is a strong tower; the righteous runs into it and is safe" (Proverbs 18:10).

DEVOTIONAL READING
BY JOHN HENRY JOWETT

DEAR FRIEND,

You have lived in Psalm 34 and studied how you can have hope when you need deliverance. Take some time to think about all you have learned and write a prayer to the Lord expressing all that is on your heart.

What were your most meaningful discoveries this week as you spent time with the Lord?

Most meaningful insight:

Most meaningful devotional reading:

Most meaningful verse:

In one of my garden books there is a chapter with a very arresting heading, "Flowers that grow in the gloom." It deals with those patches in a garden which never catch the sunlight, the dull corners which at no part of the day are found with shining faces. And my guide tells me the sort of flowers which are not afraid of these

---

dingy corners, nay, rather like them and flourish in them. There are plants which seem to thrive in apparent adversity…Who has not known men and women who when they arrive at seasons of gloom and solitude put on strength and hopefulness like a robe? They have lovely things to live with. They have their own old loyalties. They have sweet memories which come freighted with rich cargoes from far-off years. They have large sympathies which keep them young, and which preserve their leaf from withering. They have sunny alluring visions. And far more wonderful than all these, in their humble lot there comes another Bethlehem, in which the Lord of Glory incarnates himself in hallowing power and peace. You may imprison such folk where you please, you shut up their treasure with them. You cannot shut it out. You may make their material lot a desert, but the wilderness and the solitary place shall be glad, and the desert shall rejoice and blossom like the rose.[15]

JOHN HENRY JOWETT

Viewer Guide
‑‑‑ WEEK FIVE ‑‑‑

The Banquet Hall Of The Lord

In Week Five of *A Heart That Hopes In God* you studied Psalm 34 and learned that God is the God of deliverances. Whenever you need a rescue, you learn to run to God. Today, as we share together, I want to look together with you at the privilege all hearts that hope in God have of entering into God's banquet hall and feasting together with Him.

"O taste and see that the LORD is good; how blessed is the man who takes refuge in Him" (Psalm 34:8).

How David Would Encourage You In Your Difficulty

1. _____

Psalm 18:3

It means to lift up His _____ instead of lifting up the circumstance.

2. _____

Psalm 18:8

Where is the banquet hall of delicacies? _____
There you will taste of all the Lord's delicacies.

"Your words were found and I ate them, and Your words became for me a joy and the delight of my heart" (Jeremiah 15:16).

3. _____

Psalm 18:9

Prizing the Lord means He is _____to you.

What will happen as a result?

1. _____verse 6

2. _____verse 7

3. _____verse 8

4. _____verses 9-10

5. _____verses 17, 19

6. _____verse 18

7. _____verse 22

≈◎   *Video messages are available on DVDs or as Downloadable M4V Video. Audio messages are available on Audio CDs or as Downloadable MP3 Audio. Visit the Quiet Time Ministries Online Store at www.quiettime.org.*

HOPE WHEN YOU ARE IN DARKNESS

Psalm 91

When a train goes through a tunnel and it gets dark, you don't throw away
the ticket and jump off. You sit and trust the engineer.

CORRIE TEN BOOM

YOU DWELL IN THE SHELTER OF THE MOST HIGH

He who dwells in the shelter of the Most High…
PSALM 91:1

PREPARE YOUR HEART

When the news is devastating, the day goes wrong, the loss is overwhelming, and you experience the dark night of the soul, you can know that it's not over. Why? Because you have a shelter. And because of your shelter, hope can stand strong in the face of any storm that comes your way. Mrs. Charles Cowman tells the story of two painters in her book, Streams In The Desert. Each painter was asked to paint a picture illustrating his own idea of rest. The first chose for his scene a quiet, lonely lake, nestled among mountains far away. The second, using swift, broad strokes on his canvas, painted a thundering waterfall. Beneath the falls grew a fragile birch tree, bending over the foam. On its branches, nearly wet with the spray from the falls, sat a robin on its nest. Is it not so? The storm makes the place of protection ever so more meaningful both to the one protected and to those looking on. Hope in the storm will always begin in answer to this question, "Where do you live your life?" Do you live and dwell in the shelter of the Most High God? Today, as you draw near to the Lord, ask Him to quiet your heart and open your eyes to the powerful truths in one of the most precious psalms in all of Scripture.

READ AND STUDY GOD'S WORD

1. This week you are going to have the privilege to live in Psalm 91. The author is unknown and perhaps that is best as it places the focus on the words and makes it a source of comfort and healing balm for any who are in the trenches when it comes to the suffering of life. If you know or have known the weariness of the road of suffering, then linger here in Psalm 91 for awhile. Read Psalm 91 and record the verse or phrase that is most significant to you today.

2. What does it mean to "dwell in the shelter of the Most High?" The word "shelter" is translated "secret place" in the New King James Version and is sometimes translated "hiding place." You have a hiding place, a secret place where you can live and dwell and enjoy even though you still reside on earth. The word in the Hebrew is *seter* and means covering, protection, and hiding place. The word for "dwell" is *yashab* and means to remain, stay, or inhabit. This word for "dwell" implies that you do not come to the secret place of the Most High God as "guests to an inn, but as inhabitants to a safe dwelling place" where you can live securely."[1] In the name of God, El Elyon, translated as "Most High," you see the supremacy of your Lord. There is no other. He reigns supreme—He is the Most High God. And as the Most High God, He looms so large on the landscape of your life when you live in Him and He is your shelter and hiding place in such a way that the storms of life, though they may get you wet, will not keep you from God's purpose and plan. You can know that even in the storm He is your protection. Spurgeon points out that "the blessings here promised are not for all believers, but for those who live in close fellowship with God." He goes on to say, "Every child of God looks towards the inner sanctuary and the mercy-seat, yet all do not dwell in the most holy place; they run to it at times, and enjoy occasional approaches, but they do not habitually reside in the mysterious presence."[2] The condition is set forth from the beginning, "He who dwells in the shelter of the Most High…"

As you think about all of this, describe in your own words what you think it means to dwell in the shelter of the Most High.

3. Look at the following verses and record what you learn about your hiding place, your shelter in the Lord.

Psalm 17:8

Psalm 27:5

Psalm 31:20

Psalm 64:2

ADORE GOD IN PRAYER

Pray the words of F.B. Meyer today: "Lift me up, by your strong arm, above the mists and darkness of the valley, to stand and walk with you on the high level of your presence and glory."[3]

YIELD YOURSELF TO GOD

Long ago a man sought the perfect picture of peace. Not finding one that satisfied, he announced a contest to produce this masterpiece. The challenge stirred the imagination of artists everywhere, and paintings arrived from far and wide. Finally the great day of revelation arrived. The judges uncovered one peaceful scene after another, while the viewers clapped and cheered. The tensions grew. Only two pictures remained veiled. As a judge pulled the cover from one, a hush fell over the crowd. A mirror-smooth lake reflected lacy, green birches under the soft blush of the evening sky. Along the grassy shore, a flock of sheep grazed undisturbed. Surely this was the winner. The man with the vision uncovered the second painting himself, and the crowd gasped in surprise. Could this be peace? A tumultuous waterfall cascaded down a rocky precipice; the crowd could almost feel its cold, penetrating spray. Stormy-gray clouds threatened to explode with lightning, wind and rain. In the midst of the thundering noises and bitter chill, a spindly tree clung to the rocks at the edge of the falls. One of its branches reached out in front of the torrential waters as if foolishly seeking to experience its full power. A little bird had built a nest in the elbow of that branch. Content and undisturbed in her stormy surroundings, she rested on her eggs. With her eyes closed and her wings ready to cover her little ones, she manifested peace that transcends all earthly turmoil.[4]

BERIT KJOS IN A WARDROBE FROM THE KING

ENJOY HIS PRESENCE

Have you discovered what it is to enjoy that close fellowship with your Lord—the shelter of the Most High? Will you resolve each day to step away from the crowd and take time to sit with Him, open the pages of His Word, hear what He has to say, and talk "heart to heart" with Him? Close your time by writing a prayer to the Lord expressing all that is on your heart. God bless you today.

REST IN HIS LOVE

"Keep me as the apple of the eye; hide me in the shadow of your wings" (Psalm 17:8).

YOU ABIDE IN THE SHADOW
OF THE ALMIGHTY

...will abide in the shadow of the Almighty.
PSALM 91:1

PREPARE YOUR HEART

It was a dark day when Elisabeth Elliot received the news that her precious husband would not be returning home from the mission trip to the Curaray River deep in the jungle of Ecuador. He, along with 4 other missionaries, was killed by the Auca Indians, the very tribe they were trying to reach with the gospel. It was a surprise attack as it had initially appeared that the missionaries were actually making progress in reaching this unreached group of people in the heart of Ecuador. The picture of the missionary wives, including Elisabeth Elliot, receiving the shocking news, tells the whole story of the darkness of the hour.

And all who are precious to God have a dark hour. According to Jesus, there is no exemption from such storms that wage war with our very soul. He promised His disciples, "I have told you all this so that you may have peace in me. Here on earth you will have many trials and sorrows. But take heart, because I have overcome the world" (John 16:33 NLT).

As you begin your quiet time, ask God to speak to you from His Word and show you what it means to "abide in the shadow of the Almighty."

READ AND STUDY GOD'S WORD

1. Begin your time in the Word of God today by reading Psalm 91:1. Then write this verse out word-for-word in the space provided.

2. This verse tells us that those who dwell in the shelter of the Most High "will abide in the shadow of the Almighty." It's a promise. Notice that little word, "will." Little words are sometimes the largest words. In this case it signifies a promise from God. The word "abide" means to "lodge" or "spend the night." The word "shadow" implies that the very Presence of the Almighty God Himself, El Shaddai, is with you. You are "spending the night" under the shadow of El Shaddai, the God who is All-Sufficient One who gives you everything you need for every circumstance of life. That's what His name, El Shaddai, tells you about His character. And then remember, all of this is a singular promise to the one who "dwells in the shelter of the Most High"; the one who lives in close fellowship with God. What truth about God means the most to you right now in light of all you are experiencing in your own life?

3. A shadow often casts a darkness. But when it is the shadow of El Shaddai, then there can be a blessing in that darkness. Read Isaiah 45:2-3, words from the Lord to Cyrus. They are words that reveal a powerful truth about the darkness we may face in life. You may want to look at these words in your Bible as well and underline what is most important to you.

> "I will go before you and make the rough places smooth;
> I will shatter the doors of bronze and cut through their iron bars.
> I will give you the treasures of darkness
> And hidden wealth of secret places,
> So that you may know that it is I,
> The LORD, the God of Israel,
> who calls you by your name."

4. What have you learned about abiding in the shadow of the Almighty that you can carry with you today?

ADORE GOD IN PRAYER

O God, Thou art our God, and therefore do we seek unto Thee. We have a covenant interest in Thee. Thou hast given Thyself to us of old in the person of Thy dear Son. Thou art our Surety. Thou, O Saviour, didst stand for us in the transactions of eternity. Thou didst also redeem us in the fullness of time, laying down Thy life that we might live, and now Thou art All-in-All to us. Our life is not in ourselves, but in Thee. Our truest and best self is Christ, for we live not, save only as our 'life is hid with Christ in God.' Lord, we want to enter into closest possible fellowship with Thyself. In days gone by Thou hast cast Thy skirt over Thy servants. In the shadow of Thy wing we have rejoiced. In the light of Thy countenance we have been ready to die of excessive joy. The coming near to us of our God has been heaven, it is indeed all the heaven we expect in the future, as it is all we have known in the past. Come near, O our God, come nearer, nearer, nearer. Still some secret to our heart reveal, as yet undiscovered. Thou hast led some of us into darkness and not into light, and thou hast covered us in the night watches and made it darkness round about us, till our spirit sank within us. Now it is Thy way to bring light out of darkness, and joy out of sorrow…O that the sorrow pang might bring forth today in Thy people some new joys, some blessed novelty of fellowship, that we may enter yet more and more into the secret places and tabernacles of the Most High, and dwell beneath the shadow of the Almighty. O Lord, Thy people want this; nothing can strengthen, comfort, lighten, sanctify and perfect us as this. Are we earth bound? Oh for Thy presence, and we shall be of a heavenly mind. Are we deeply depressed in spirit? Oh, for the light of Thy countenance, for it shall make us gladder than a wedding day. Oh that we might get at Thee, our God, for then shall the bonds of this world seem like cobwebs and disappear.[5]

CHARLES HADDON SPURGEON IN BEHOLD THE THRONE OF GRACE

YIELD YOURSELF TO GOD

What do these men and women find in their dark experiences which makes them sing like nightingales in gloomy woods? Do they make any discoveries in the darkness which explains their joy? Yes, that is the secret, they have some supremely precious findings which make reproach and persecution seem like nothing. What do they discover? They have the wonderful joy of discovering God in more and more of His glory. The dark places become the home of vision. They find their eyes in the night, and they penetrate the veil of the darkness and see the Lord…But there is another discovery which they make in their darkness. They have the joy of discovering other souls, and winning them to the Lord. There are some folk who are only found through the medium of dark experiences. If we never suffered they would never be won. The revelation made through suffering becomes a constraint which they cannot resist. What I mean is this; we see some man's noble bearing under reproach, and the splendid testimony lays its grip upon us. A brave and radiant endurance makes conquests of many men who would be unmoved by words spoken in sunny circumstances. It is the encircling gloom which makes the testimony glorious. I verily believe that Stephen's magnificent bearing in the night laid hold of Saul of Tarsus and would not let him go. Saul never got away from it, and it coloured his thought and life to the very end.[6]

JOHN HENRY JOWETT IN LIFE IN THE HEIGHTS

ENJOY HIS PRESENCE

Friend, do you dwell in the shelter of the Most High and abide in the shadow of the Almighty? Do you see the promise given to those who enjoy close fellowship with the Lord? Close by writing a prayer to the Lord expressing all that is on your heart today.

REST IN HIS LOVE

"And I will give you treasures hidden in the darkness—secret riches. I will do this so you may know that I am the LORD, the God of Israel, the one who calls you by name" (Isaiah 45:3).

YOU TRUST IN YOUR REFUGE AND FORTRESS

I will say to the LORD, "My refuge and my fortress, My God, in whom I trust!"
PSALM 91:2

PREPARE YOUR HEART

Theodore Beza, born in Vezelay, France in 1519 attended the University of Orleans and received a degree in law. He had a passion for culture and poetry, worldly success and fame, and found that the faith he had embraced earlier in his life was plagued with doubt. When he suffered a critical illness, his faith and love for God and His Word was revived, and he moved to Geneva. In 1548, he attended a Reformed Assembly church service and the congregation sang Psalm 91. Beza never forgot the profound effect those words had in his heart, "I will say of the Lord, He is my refuge and my fortress: my God; in Him will I trust." He felt a new strength and courage to meet any danger that came his way. He became a lifelong friend of John Calvin and when Calvin died, Beza succeeded him as head of the Genevan Church and leader of the Calvinist movement in Europe. At the end of his life, he told those who were with him that in the midst of all the changes of his life, he had found God to be faithful to fulfill all the promises of God, one by one.

The bright truth of today is that even in times of darkness, the Lord is your refuge and fortress and, best of all, you can trust Him. As a preparation of heart, meditate on these words by Amy Carmichael:

God of the deeps, how near Thou art;
Here are Thy garments: sea and shore.
Beauty of all things show in part
Thee whom, unseen, we love, adore.
Thine are the good salt winds that blow;
Thine is the magic of the sea;
Glories of color from Thee flow—
We worship Thee, we worship Thee.

God of the tempest and the calm,
God of the tireless, patient tides,
God of the water's healing balm,
And gentle sounds where stillness bides,
God of the stainless fields of blue,
God of the grandeur of the sea,
Swifter than ever spindrift flew,
Like homing birds, we fly to Thee.

God of the waves that roll and swell
And break in tossing clouds of foam
Thy handiwork the painted shell;
For fragile life how safe a home.
God of the great, and of the small,
God of the glory of the sea,
Here in the quiet evenfall
We worship Thee, we worship Thee.[7]

AMY CARMICHAEL IN MOUNTAIN BREEZES

READ AND STUDY GOD'S WORD

1. To have a heart that hopes in God it is essential that the heart can trust in Him. David tells us something important about trust. He says, "The LORD also will be a stronghold for the oppressed, a stronghold in times of trouble; and those who know Your name will put their trust in You, for You, O LORD, have not forsaken those who seek You" (Psalm 9:9-10). Names of God reveal His Person and Character. When you know God firsthand in your own experience of a personal dynamic intimate abundant relationship with Him, then as you grow in that intimate knowledge of Him, you will trust Him. To trust Him means that you rely on Him in stress and trial. Trusting Him is your first reliance, not your last resort. What can you know about your God that will help you trust in Him? One of the best places to make these essential discoveries is in the Psalms. Every psalm has powerful truths about God. Learn to keep your eyes open for these truths and then, write them down, memorize them, and never let them go. Look at the following verses and record what you learn about God:

Psalm 3:3

Psalm 16:11

Psalm 23:1

Psalm 27:1

Psalm 28:7-8

Psalm 46:1

2. What is the most important truth you have learned about God today that will help you trust Him more in the dark times of life?

ADORE GOD IN PRAYER

Look at all that you learned about God today. Thank the Lord for each truth you've learned about Him today. Then, lay all your burdens at His feet.

YIELD YOURSELF TO GOD

A spiritual kingdom lies all about us, enclosing us, embracing us, altogether within reach of our inner selves, waiting for us to recognize it. God Himself is here waiting our response to His Presence. This eternal world will come alive to us the moment we begin to reckon upon its reality...What do I mean by reality? I mean that which has existence apart from any idea any mind may have of it, and which would exist if there were no mind anywhere to entertain a thought of it. That which is real has being in itself. It does not depend upon the observer for its validity…As we begin to focus upon God the things of the spirit will take shape before our inner eyes. Obedience to the word of Christ will bring an inward revelation of the Godhead (John 14:21-23). It will give acute perception enabling us to see God even as is promised to the pure in heart. A new God-consciousness will seize upon us and we shall begin to taste and hear and inwardly feel the God who is our life and our all. There will be seen the constant shining of the light that lighteth every man that cometh into the world. More and more, as our faculties grow sharper and more sure, God will become to us the great All, and His Presence the glory and wonder of our lives.[8]

A.W. Tozer in The Pursuit Of God

ENJOY HIS PRESENCE

God can be known and He can be trusted. Close your time today by thinking about the benefits of trusting the Lord seen in these words by Jeremiah, "Blessed is the man who trusts in the LORD and whose trust is the LORD. For he will be like a tree planted by the water that extends its roots by a stream and will not fear when the heat comes; but its leaves will be green, and it will not be anxious in a year of drought nor cease to yield fruit" (Jeremiah 17:17-8). Always remember that the first line of that beloved hymn is so true: *Tis so sweet to trust in Jesus.* Close by writing a prayer to the Lord expressing all that is on your heart.

REST IN HIS LOVE

"And they who know Your name [who have experience and acquaintance with Your mercy] will lean on and confidently put their trust in You, for You, Lord, have not forsaken those who seek(inquire of and for) You [on the authority of God's Word and the right of their necessity]" (Psalm 9:10 AMP).

⊰⊱ **DAY 4** *⊰⊱*

YOU HIDE UNDER HIS WINGS

He will cover you with his feathers. He will shelter you with his wings. His faithful promises are your armor and protection.

PSALM 91:4 NLT

PREPARE YOUR HEART

In 1752 Katharina A. von Schlegel wrote the words of a hymn that has been sung by thousands as a comfort and hope in their own dark times. This hymn was said to be a favorite of Eric Liddell, the athlete who became known for refusing to run in the 1924 Olympics on the Sabbath. He later became a missionary in China and was imprisoned during World War II where he later died. He was said to be the joy of that prison camp and taught the words of this beloved hymn to those who were suffering there. Meditate on the words of this hymn as a preparation of heart today. If you know the melody you might sing the words to the Lord.

> Be still, my soul: the Lord is on thy side.
>
> Bear patiently the cross of grief or pain.
>
> Leave to thy God to order and provide;
>
> In every change, He faithful will remain.
>
> Be still, my soul: thy best, thy heavenly Friend
>
> Through thorny ways leads to a joyful end.
>
>
> Be still, my soul: thy God doth undertake
>
> To guide the future, as He has the past.
>
> Thy hope, thy confidence let nothing shake;
>
> All now mysterious shall be bright at last.
>
> Be still, my soul: the waves and winds still know
>
> His voice Who ruled them while He dwelt below.

Be still, my soul: when dearest friends depart,

And all is darkened in the vale of tears,

Then shalt thou better know His love, His heart,

Who comes to soothe thy sorrow and thy fears.

Be still, my soul: thy Jesus can repay

From His own fullness all He takes away.

Be still, my soul: the hour is hastening on

When we shall be forever with the Lord.

When disappointment, grief and fear are gone,

Sorrow forgot, love's purest joys restored.

Be still, my soul: when change and tears are past

All safe and blessed we shall meet at last.

Be still, my soul: begin the song of praise

On earth, be leaving, to Thy Lord on high;

Acknowledge Him in all thy words and ways,

So shall He view thee with a well pleased eye.

Be still, my soul: the Sun of life divine

Through passing clouds shall but more brightly shine.

READ AND STUDY GOD'S WORD

1. There is a beautiful picture, a metaphor, in this psalm that tells you something very important about your Lord, something that can be lifechanging if you do not yet know it. The Lord is the One who has chosen to give us a metaphor that we might understand the mother instinct that resides in Him to protect those who belong to Him. It is the picture of a mother bird who cherishes and protects her young. If you have ever seen a mother quail with all her baby quail (chicks) then you know the watchful care she gives to her brood. But there is even more in this picture. A mother hen will spread out her large wings and gather her chicks close to her. The feathers of her

wings keep those chicks warm and secure. This is a picture of love, care, safety and security. Read Psalm 91:4-9. What is your favorite verse or phrase in this passage of Scripture today?

2. Read Isaiah 49:15-16 and write your insights about what these verses tell you about your Lord: "Can a woman forget her nursing child and have no compassion on the son of her womb? Even these may forget, but I will not forget you. Behold, I have inscribed you on the palms of My hands; Your walls are continually before Me."

3. In a time of darkness in life, how is this truth about God an encouragement?

ADORE GOD IN PRAYER

How do you need to hide under the wings of the Lord today? Draw near to Him now and talk with Him about it. Be still and know that He is God (Psalm 46:10 NIV).

YIELD YOURSELF TO GOD

God is our refuge and strength, a very present help in trouble (Psalm 46:1). When your trials were so severe that you were forced to flee to God, did you find this statement true? His door was never closed. He never said, "Go elsewhere." He never upbraided you for presumption when you came. When you hid in Him, it was a blessed retreat. When you entered your closet, shut the door, and hid with God, you had perfect peace. Look at the little chicks under the hen. See how they bury their heads in the feathers of her warm bosom. Hear their little chirps of perfect happiness as they nestle under their mother's wing. "He shall cover you with His feathers, and under His wings you shall take refuge; His truth shall be your shield and buckler" (Ps. 91:4). Have you found this to be true? My happiest hours have not been days of pleasure but nights of sorrow. When all waters are bitter, the cup of divine consolation is all the sweeter. For brightness, do not give me sunshine, give me the Lord's superior glory, for it lights up affliction's darkness. Happiness does not depend on success in business or being applauded by one and all. The only thing necessary for happiness is for the Lord to smile on you. It is not essential to be in good health or even naturally cheerful. God gives the truest health in sickness and the most tender joy in depression. "God is our refuge and strength, a very present help in trouble" (Ps. 46:1). It has been many days since we first went to Him, and we have been many times since, but He has never failed. To know Him is life eternal. To know Him is solid peace. No calamity can destroy that peace.[9]

CHARLES HADDON SPURGEON IN BESIDE STILL WATERS

ENJOY HIS PRESENCE

The powerful truth here is that God is your hiding place and your protector. The writers of the psalms knew this and you can know it too. "You are my hiding place and my shield. I wait for Your word" (Psalm 119:114). "You are my hiding place; You preserve me from trouble; You surround me with songs of deliverance" (Psalm 32:7). When you find yourself in a time of darkness, find hope in the truth that you can hide under His wings and find warmth and security in His faithfulness. Close by writing a prayer in your journal expressing all that is on your heart.

REST IN HIS LOVE

"God is our refuge and strength, a very present help in trouble. Therefore we will not fear, though the earth should change and though the mountains slip into the heart of the sea" (Psalm 46:1-2).

YOU REST IN A SECURE PLACE ON HIGH

Because he has loved Me, therefore I will deliver him; I will set
him securely on high, because he has known My name.

PSALM 91:14

PREPARE YOUR HEART

One of the great challenges in the Christian life is the dilemma of verses that seem to say you will never experience pain. Always take into account the whole counsel of God's Word. The Bible also promises trial. Two examples are Job and Jesus. Both suffered the dark night of the soul. Job finally surrendered to God in the midst of his trial by saying, "Though He slay me, yet I will trust Him." Jesus cried out, "Yet not my will, but Thine be done." And so, how are we to understand, "Because he has loved Me, therefore I will deliver him" (Psalm 91:14)? The psalmist who wrote Psalm 91 discovered that God had "set him securely on high." Paul discovered this as well when he wrote, "But God, being rich in mercy, because of His great love with which He loved us, even when we were dead in our transgressions, made us alive together with Christ (by grace you have been saved), and raised us up with Him, and seated us with Him in the heavenly places in Christ Jesus, so that in the ages to come He might show the surpassing riches of His grace in kindness toward us in Christ Jesus" (Ephesians 2:6). Because of where we are positionally residing, we may, in a sense, touch heaven when we are tested by fire. Ask God to show you these truths today and help you in applying them to your life. As you begin your quiet time, meditate on the words of this hymn by Charles Gabriel (1856-1932), then write a prayer asking the Lord to speak to you today:

I stand amazed in the presence of Jesus the Nazarene,

And wondered how He could love me, A sinner condemned, unclean.

How Marvelous how wonderful! And my song shall ever be;

How Marvelous how wonderful! Is my Savior's love for me!

READ AND STUDY GOD'S WORD

1. It is clear that while we are on earth, there are going to be times of loss, suffering, grieving, and dark trial. We have been given a glimpse of the trial of Jesus in Gethsemane and on the cross. We also know from the writer of Hebrews that Jesus "for the joy set before Him endured the cross, despising the shame, and has sat down at the right hand of the throne of God" (Hebrews 12:2). There was something not clearly visible to others that Jesus saw—a "joy" set before Him that enabled Him to endure the cross. There was deliverance in the trial because of that joy. You can know that there are eternal truths for you in God's Word that transcend the boundary of time that no amount of suffering can touch. These are the truths that give you hope and deliverance in the midst of trouble and darkness. They are the truths that enable you to touch heaven while tested by fire. Paul said, "For momentary light affliction is producing for us an eternal weight of glory far beyond all comparison, while we look not at the things which are seen, but at the things which are not seen; for the things which are seen are temporal, but the things which are not seen are eternal" (2 Corinthians 4:17-18). What is your favorite insight in what you've just read that means the most to you today?

2. Look at the following verses and write out the truths that can help you in a time of trial:

Ephesians 1:3-12

Philippians 4:13, 19

Colossians 3:1-4

ADORE GOD IN PRAYER

Psalm 91:15 promises "He will call upon Me, and I will answer him; I will be with him in trouble; I will rescue him and honor him." Call upon Him today with all that is on your heart.

YIELD YOURSELF TO GOD

"Hath raised us up together, and made us sit together in heavenly places in Christ Jesus" (Eph. 2:6). The important question is, Where are you living? On which level do you normally reside? Are you experientially living in the "heavenly places" day by day? The Lord Jesus meant just that when He said, "Abide in Me." Abide means to stay where you are. Positionally, you are there. Rest in your blessed portion, in the One who is your life, by faith in the facts. Your two mortal enemies, Satan and the old man, will seek to drag you down in spirit — down into the sense realm, into depression, under circumstances or conditions. But your rightful position is on top; therefore, refuse to come down. Never be governed by your fluctuating feelings. What is true concerning your justification is also true regarding your sanctification. Feelings do not count! It is your Father's fact that matters. Assert and affirm your position by faith in the completed work.

I was much impressed some years ago, at a Missionary Conference, to hear an aged missionary, recently home from the field, assert that she had often longed to know this heavenly position, but had never been able to get there — or, as she expressed it, to get "within the veil." One of the leaders present was able to take her to the Word at Ephesians 2:6. He explained that in the purpose of her Father she was already there. This was the Father's fact. There was no need to strive for a position that was already hers. "You are there; believe it, and take your position, by simple faith in the Word." It was a joy to see the glow that came into her face, and her blessed release as she recognized that simple truth for the first time, after forty years on the foreign field. It is not an act to be performed, or an ideal to be realized, but a fact to be believed. It is not a promise to be pleaded or claimed, or appropriated, but an established truth to be rested in.

When distributing tracts in a village in the Yorkshire dales, some distance from the railway station, a Christian worker entered the dwelling of a dear old saint of God, eighty-four years of age, who lived there alone. One room was all she occupied, and everything in it bespoke the most abject poverty. If the contents of her abode had been knocked down at the auctioneer's hammer, the whole of it would not have fetched more than five shillings.

Being desirous of cheering and comforting his aged friend, he remarked to her: "Well, Margaret, soon we shall have done for ever with the trials and difficulties of the way and be fully happy with the blessed Lord Jesus up yonder." "That's my home now, sir," she replied. Finding he had begun much below the mark, he sped on, with a view of helping her if possible, and said, "Yes, Margaret, soon we shall be in that bright Home, that Father's house above, with the Lord Jesus, rejoicing ever in His presence." "I live there now, sir," was her bright and smiling reply. Finding himself still very considerably in the rear, he hastened on to say, "How blessed it will be, Margaret — will it not? — when we and all the redeemed are praising Him together in the glory forever!" "I sing there every night, sir," was her joyous response. Thus his expectations were far more than realized; for instead of helping "poor" Margaret, he was instructed and helped himself.[10]

REGINALD WALLIS IN THE COMPLETE WORKS OF MILES J. STANFORD

ENJOY HIS PRESENCE

To live by the eternal truths given to us in the Bible is to rest in the heavenly places, day by day, with your Lord. You have the ultimate hope that no one can ever take from you and that is, that your place with the Lord in heaven is secure. Nothing and no one can touch that. Eternal life is a promise for all who receive Christ and surrender their life to Him. "By grace you have been saved through faith; and that not of yourselves, it is the gift of God; not as a result of works, so that no one may boast" (Ephesians 2:8-9). If you have never received Christ and established a relationship, you may do so by praying a prayer like this: *Lord Jesus, I need You. Thank You for dying on the cross for my sins. I ask You now to come into my life, forgive my sins, and make me the person You want me to be. In Jesus' name, Amen.* Having received Christ, all the promises of God are yours. Do you know them? Open the pages of the Bible and live there so that you can live out each day with heaven in mind even when you are tested by the dark night of the soul. You will find that you will be able to say along with the hymnwriter, "I stand amazed in the Presence of Jesus the Nazarene!"

REST IN HIS LOVE

"Therefore if you have been raised up with Christ, keep seeking the things above, where Christ is, seated at the right hand of God. Set your mind on the things above, not on the things that are on earth. For you have died and your life is hidden with Christ in God. When Christ, who is our life, is revealed, then you also will be revealed with Him in glory" (Colossians 3:1-4).

DEVOTIONAL READING
BY KENNETH WUEST

DEAR FRIEND,

Think about all you have learned this week in Psalm 91 about finding hope when you are in darkness. Write a prayer to the Lord thanking Him for all that He is teaching you.

What were your most meaningful discoveries this week as you spent time with the Lord?

Most meaningful insight:

Most meaningful devotional reading:

Most meaningful verse:

The things that hedge us in, the things that handicap us, the tests that we go through and the temptations that assail us, are all divinely appointed wood cutters used by God to hew out a path for our preaching of the gospel. It may be that our fondest hopes are not realized. We are in difficult circumstances. Illness may be our lot. Yet if we are in the center of God's will, all these are contributing to the progress of the gospel. They draw us closer to the Lord so that the testimony of our lives will count more for God, and thus we become more efficient in proclaiming the gospel. Thank God for the handicaps and the testings. They are blessings in disguise. When we have limitations imposed upon us we do our best work for the Lord, for then we are most dependent upon Him. Paul said, "Most gladly therefore will I rather glory in my infirmities, that the power of Christ may rest upon me" (2 Cor. 12:9). Paul knew then, for he had plenty of them.[11]

KENNETH WUEST IN WUEST'S WORD STUDIES

Viewer Guide

Have You Made The Big Move?

In Week Six of *A Heart That Hopes In God*, you had the opportunity to study Psalm 91, one of the great and comforting psalms in the Bible. Today I want to ask you the question, "Where do you live in life?" You are going to discover that living in the shelter of the Most High, following the example of the writer of Psalm 91, requires a big move. Grab your Bibles, and let's dig in more deeply together as we study the powerful truths of Psalm 91.

"He who dwells in the shelter of the Most High will abide in the shadow of the Almighty" (Psalm 91:1).

A. We must make the big move from _____ to _____.

Psalm 91:2

Trust is *batah* and means reliance or confidence and results in safety or security from relying on God.

Trust can be understood to mean: "I hang my heart on You Lord." (United Bible Society)

B. To make the big move requires _____ and _____.

Psalm 91:2

Faith is a _____ and a _____.

How do you pack your bags and get ready for your big move?

1. Make a decisive, intentional _____ about the Bible.

2._____ the most important, relevant promises for you from the Bible.

3. Make faith in God's Word a _____of your life. Begin to
_____your faith.

4. Recognize _____of faith as opportunities for your faith to grow.

Where will you live when you make this move?

C. You will live in the _____of the Lord.

≈≈ *Video messages are available on DVDs or as Downloadable M4V Video. Audio messages are available on Audio CDs or as Downloadable MP3 Audio. Visit the Quiet Time Ministries Online Store at www.quiettime.org.*

Week Seven

HOPE WHEN YOU NEED HELP

Psalm 121

There is never a time when we may not hope in God. Whatever our necessities, however great our difficulties, and though to all appearances help is impossible, yet our business is to hope in God, and it will be found that it is not in vain. In the Lord's own time help will come. Oh, the hundreds, yea, the thousands of times that I have found it thus within the past seventy years and four months!

GEORGE MUELLER

LIFT UP YOUR EYES

I will lift up my eyes to the mountains; from where shall my help come?
PSALM 121:1

PREPARE YOUR HEART

Hope throughout your life, especially in a time when you need help, is dependent on where you look and what you see. Jesus said, "The eye is the lamp of the body" (Matthew 6:22). The psalmist has said, How blessed are the people who know the joyful sound! O LORD, they walk in the light of Your countenance. In Your name they rejoice all the day, and by Your righteousness they are exalted. For You are the glory of their strength…" (Psalm 89:15-17). Corrie ten Boom spoke often of an experience at Ravensbruck concentration camp that occurred during their 4:30 am roll call. Life was intolerable and yet the Lord was at work even at one of the darkest places on earth. During one particular roll call a cruel prison guard kept everyone standing a long time to increase the depth of their suffering and pain. Suddenly a skylark began to sing in the sky, and all the prisoners looked up. When Corrie looked at the bird her eyes moved beyond to the sky and she immediately thought of Psalm 103:11, "For as high as the heavens are above the earth, so great is His lovingkindness toward those who fear Him." In that moment, Corrie saw that God's love is greater than the deepest hate of man. The Lord sent that skylark to Ravensbruck during roll call for three weeks, effectively turning the eyes of those prisoners from hate to the ocean of God's love. Corrie ten Boom experienced what the psalmist speaks of in Psalm 121; The travel of the eye moved from the circumstance to the Lord. Ask God today to teach you how to lift up your eyes to Him in every situation.

READ AND STUDY GOD'S WORD

1. Today you begin a journey in a psalm that you will return to time and time again in your life. It is one that has brought hope to countless unnamed believers. Read Psalm 121 and write your most significant insight.

2. Write out Psalm 121:1 word-for-word in the space provided.

3. Read the following verses and record all that you learn about where to "look" with your eyes:

Psalm 25:15-20

Psalm 123:1-2

Psalm 141:8

4. Describe ways that you can "lift up" your eyes to the Lord, moving from being consumed with feelings and circumstances to focus on the Lord.

ADORE GOD IN PRAYER

One of the great prayers is to ask the Lord to help you lift your eyes up to Him. Is there anything you need to look away from? Take each troubling circumstance, person, or feeling to the Lord. Very often He will send a "skylark" your way in the form of a person or some other messenger to help you look up in your situation. Look for His hand at work in your life.

YIELD YOURSELF TO GOD

Help comes to saints only from above, they look elsewhere in vain, let us lift up our eyes with hope, expectancy, desire and confidence. Satan will endeavour to keep our eyes upon our sorrows that we may be disquieted and discouraged; be it ours firmly to resolve that we will look out and look up, for there is good cheer for the eyes, and they that lift up their eyes to the eternal hills shall soon have their hearts lifted up also. The purposes of God; the divine attributes; the immutable promises; the covenant, ordered in all things and sure; the providence, predestination, and proved faithfulness of the Lord—these are the hills to which we must lift our eyes, for from these our help must come. It is our resolve that we will not be bandaged and blindfolded, but will lift up our eyes.[1]

CHARLES HADDON SPURGEON IN THE TREASURY OF DAVID

ENJOY HIS PRESENCE

Corrie ten Boom used to say:

"Focus on the world around you and you'll be DISTRESSED.
Focus on yourself and you'll be DEPRESSED.
But focus on your God and you'll be REFRESHED and at REST."

The secret in those times when you are in great need is to lift up your eyes to the plans and purposes of God, to the Word, and ultimately to the Lord, where you have a clear view of His Person and Character. As you close your time with the Lord, write out the most important truth you have learned that you can carry with you throughout the day.

REST IN HIS LOVE

"My eyes are continually toward the LORD, for He will pluck my feet out of the net" (Psalm 25:15).

DAY 2

YOU HAVE A HELPER

My help comes from the LORD, Who made heaven and earth.
PSALM 121:2

PREPARE YOUR HEART

What are you to do in a situation where there is seemingly no one to help? Even when there is no earthly help, there is heavenly help for you. This help is from the Lord Himself. Imagine the circumstance of Corrie and Betsie ten Boom, imprisoned at Ravensbruck, seemingly lost and forgotten by the whole world. Have you ever felt like that? As though you are in a far corner of the world and there is no one who knows your plight and no one who can help. Today, as you lift up your eyes to the mountains you are going to discover your Lord, an ever present help in times of trouble.

Begin your time with the Lord meditating on the words of this puritan prayer. Underline your favorite phrases:

SOVEREIGN COMMANDER OF THE UNIVERSE,
I am sadly harassed by doubts, fears, unbelief,
in a felt spiritual darkness.
My heart is full of evil surmisings and disquietude,
and I cannot act faith at all.
My heavenly pilot has disappeared,
and I have lost my hold on the rock of ages;
I sink in deep mire beneath storms and waves,
in horror and distress unutterable.
Help me, O Lord,
to throw myself absolutely and wholly on thee,
for better, for worse, without comfort, and all but hopeless.
Give me peace of soul, confidence, enlargement of mind,
morning joy that comes after night heaviness;
Water my soul richly with divine blessings;
Grant that I may welcome thy humbling in private

181

so that I might enjoy thee in public;

Give me a mountain top as high as the valley is low.

Thy grace can melt the worst sinner, and I am as vile as he;

Yet thou hast made me a monument of mercy,

a trophy of redeeming power;

In my distress let me not forget this.

All-wise God,

Thy never-failing providence orders every event,

sweetens every fear,

reveals evil's presence lurking in seeming good,

brings real good out of seeming evil,

makes unsatisfactory what I set my heart upon,

to show me what a short-sighted creature I am,

and to teach me to live by faith upon thy blessed self.

Out of my sorrow and night

give me the name Naphtali—"satisfied with favour"—

help me to love thee as thy child,

and to walk worthy of my heavenly pedigree.[2]

THE VALLEY OF VISION

READ AND STUDY GOD'S WORD

1. In Psalm 121, the psalmist's great need is for someone to help. The question from the psalmist and the question that comes to our hearts in a crisis is, "From where shall my help come?" The Hebrew word for "help" is *ezer* and means divine aid and assistance, both materially and spiritually. The answer for the psalmist is, "My help comes from the LORD, who made heaven and earth" (Psalm 121:2). Read Psalm 121 again and write out all the reasons why the Lord is a "help."

2. Read the following verses and record what you learn about the Lord's help in your life. Personalize what you learn i.e. "the Lord is my strength."

Psalm 28:7

Psalm 86:17

Psalm 107:12-16

ADORE GOD IN PRAYER

Where in your life do you need help? Turn to your prayer pages and write out all your needs and lay them out before the Lord. Be sure to date each request and watch eagerly to see how the Lord answers your prayer.

YIELD YOURSELF TO GOD

My help comes from the Lord!—The term applied to the Lord, as Creator of heaven and earth indicates his inexhaustible abundance of help. Despair is madness in anyone who has such a God to help him.[3]

F.B. MEYER IN CHOICE NOTES ON THE PSALMS

ENJOY HIS PRESENCE

David surely knew what it was to feel a great need for help when he cried out to God in Psalm 22:11, "Be not far from me, for trouble is near; for there is none to help." Corrie and Betsie ten Boom also knew it in Ravensbruck and they were helped by the Lord. The Lord helped them in that concentration camp, day-by-day in the details of their desperate trial, and opened many doors of ministry to other women. At the end of a long ten hour work detail each day, Corrie or Betsie would teach from the Bible, and the women would gather around in the dimly lit room to hear words of hope. The Lord, their helper, was at work in their lives. And He is at work in your life as well. Help will often come from an unexpected corner of your life. Watch eagerly for your God to answer the cries of your heart. No wonder David said, "In the morning, O LORD, You will hear my voice; In the morning I will order my prayer to You and eagerly watch" (Psalm 5:3) and "For You I wait all the day" (Psalm 25:5). Close your quiet time by writing a prayer to the Lord expressing all that is on your heart.

REST IN HIS LOVE

"The LORD is my strength and my shield; my heart trusts in Him and I am helped; Therefore my heart exults, and with my song I shall thank Him" (Psalm 28:7).

HE IS YOUR KEEPER

The Lord is your keeper...
PSALM 121:5

PREPARE YOUR HEART

Is there not someone who will watch over you to protect, guard, watch over, and guide you? The answer is yes! The Lord—He is your keeper. What does that mean? Today you are going to think more deeply about your Lord, Who He is, and what He does in your life. These are the kinds of truths that God often reveals to you through His choice servants, the psalmists. In fact, whenever you are in a psalm, you can always look for truths about God and what He does in your life. The psalmists were faithful to write of their firsthand experience with the Lord and as they passed it on, you too may enjoy firsthand experience of a dynamic, intimate, vibrant relationship with your Lord. As you begin your quiet time, offer up these words to the Lord from Psalm 25:16-21.

> "Turn to me and be gracious to me,
>   for I am lonely and afflicted.
> The troubles of my heart are enlarged;
>   Bring me out of my distresses.
> Look upon my affliction and my trouble,
>   and forgive all my sins.
> Look upon my enemies, for they are many,
>   and they hate me with violent hatred.
> Guard my soul and deliver me;
>   Do not let me be ashamed, for I take refuge in You.
> Let integrity and uprightness preserve me,
>   For I wait for You."

READ AND STUDY GOD'S WORD

1. In Psalm 121:5 you learn a new truth about your Lord—He is your keeper. The Hebrew word for "keeper" is *shamar* and means a guard or watchman who exercises great care over those who are being watched and guarded. In your case the Lord is watching over you and exercises

great care in doing so. Read Psalm 121 again and write out all that you learn about the Lord as your keeper.

2. The Lord keeps you and watches over you. What will that really mean for you in your life? Look at the following verses and write what you learn that will help you understand His watchfulness and care over you:

Psalm 17:6-8

Psalm 31:20-21

Psalm 66:8-12

Proverbs 5:21

ADORE GOD IN PRAYER

As you spend more and more time in Psalm 121 perhaps you are noticing that your eyes are lifted up and away from the things of this world to the things of the Lord. What are you noticing about your Lord today? Take time to praise Him for what you see about Who He is and what He does.

YIELD YOURSELF TO GOD

This beautiful Psalm is the trustful expression of a heart rejoicing in its own safety under the watchful eye of Him who is both the Maker of heaven and earth, and the Keeper of Israel. The Creator of the Universe, the Keeper of the nation, is also the Keeper of the individual. The one ever-recurring thought, the one characteristic word of the Psalm, is the word keep. Six times it is repeated in the last five verses of this one short ode—designed to mark by this emphasis of iteration the truth of God's loving care for the individual, and so to banish all shadow of doubt, fear, anxiety, lest in the vast sum the unit should be forgotten.[4]

J.J. STEWART PEROWNE IN COMMENTARY ON THE PSALMS

ENJOY HIS PRESENCE

The Lord keeps His own even in the midst of great pain and suffering experienced as we live in this temporal, fallen world. Corrie and Betsie ten Boom, imprisoned at Ravensbruck concentration camp, were ultimately both released. Betsie was granted release to a life in eternity face to face with her Lord. Corrie, through a clerical error, was set free to travel the far reaches of the earth to declare the love, forgiveness and mercy of the Lord Jesus to thousands of men and women. Corrie stepped into eternity on her birthday in 1983 at the age of 91. As you close your time with the Lord today, what is the most significant truth you have learned? Write it out in the space provided then carry it in your heart and mind throughout the day.

REST IN HIS LOVE

"We went through fire and through water, yet You brought us out into a place of abundance" (Psalm 68:12).

THE LORD IS YOUR SHADE

The LORD is your shade on your right hand.
PSALM 121:5

PREPARE YOUR HEART

On a hot day in the desert, what will bring refreshment? Shade. It's always cooler and refreshing in the shade. The Lord is your shade. In fact, Acts 3:19 tells you that "times of refreshing may come from the presence of the Lord." Oh for some coolness in the heat of a trial. That's what the presence of the Lord is for you when you are in a time of need. And so, dear friend, take heart. Search out the shade of your Lord and rest there for a few moments, even today.

READ AND STUDY GOD'S WORD

1. In Psalm 121:5 you learn that "The Lord is your shade on your right hand." F.B. Meyer says that "*Shade* is a metaphor for protection from the scorching heat...He is a shadow from the heat."[5] Isaiah also sets forth this truth: "For You have been a defense for the helpless, a defense for the needy in his distress, a refuge from the storm, a shade from the heat..." (Isaiah 25:4). Read through Psalm 121 again and describe how the Lord brings shade to you in the heat of a trial.

2. Shade brings refreshment and coolness. And so it is with the Lord. As you draw near to Him and bask in His Presence you are going to experience Him in ways that will refresh your spirit. The truth about the Lord is greater than the trial but it is difficult to see this reality when we only look at the trouble in our life. It is only as we "lift our eyes" and see Him that we can know this

powerful truth. And what then will we discover? Many powerful truths. You will discover that Jesus is the Victor in all your circumstances. Read Romans 8:31-39 and record every promise that gives you hope and brings a refreshment to your soul today.

ADORE GOD IN PRAYER

Write a prayer to the Lord in your journal expressing your love and devotion to Him.

YIELD YOURSELF TO GOD

"What makes this set of china so much more expensive than that?" asked the customer.

"It has more work on it. It has been put through the fire twice. See, in this one the flowers are in the yellow band; in that one they are on the white background. This had to be put through the fire for a second time to get the design on it."

"Why is the pattern on this vessel so blurred and marred—the design not brought out clearly?"

"That one was not burned enough. Had it remained in the furnace longer the dark background would have become gold—dazzling gold, and the pattern would have stood out clear and distinct."

Perhaps some of those who seem to have more than their share of suffering and disappointment are, like the costly china, being doubly tried in the fire, that they may be more valuable in the Master's service.

The potter never sees his clay take on rich shades of silver or red, or cream, or brown, or yellow, until after the darkness and the burning of the furnace. These colors come—after the burning and darkness. The clay is beautiful—after the burning and the darkness. The vase is made possible—after the burning and darkness.

How universal is this law of life! Where did the bravest man and the purest woman you know get their whitened characters? Did they not get them as the clay gets its beauty—after the darkness and the burning of the furnace? Where did Savonarola get his eloquence? In the darkness and burning of the furnace wherein God discovered deep things to him. Where did Stradavari get his violins? Where did Titian get his color? Where did Michelangelo get his marble? Where did Mozart get his music, and Chatterton his poetry, and Jeremiah his sermons? They got them where the clay gets its glory and its shimmer—in the darkness and the burning of the furnace.[6]

MRS. CHARLES COWMAN IN SPRINGS IN THE VALLEY

ENJOY HIS PRESENCE

Though the heat may come you can know that the purposes of God are being accomplished and the Lord has in mind a beautiful picture He is painting of your life. In the heat of today's circumstance, there is a place of shade in the presence of your Lord. Rest there, friend, in the heat of the day. In His Presence there is a time of refreshing for you.

REST IN HIS LOVE

"Times of refreshing come from the presence of the Lord…" (Acts 3:19).

ALL THE WAY TO FOREVER

The LORD will guard your going out and your coming in from this time forth and forever.

PSALM 121:8

PREPARE YOUR HEART

B oth Corrie and Betsie ten Boom are now face to face with their Lord. Spurgeon and Moody are now face to face in eternity with their God. These men and women had their brief stay on earth walking with the Lord in the realm of time and now are enjoying the privileges of "forever" with Him. Time is short and eternity is forever. Always remember that. Even Paul called affliction "momentary" and "light" when compared with the eternal weight of glory that will be ours when we step into "forever" (2 Corinthians 4:17). The great promise that is yours today is that your Lord is with you all the way to "forever."

READ AND STUDY GOD'S WORD

1. Psalm 121:8 is your focus in your quiet time today. Read that verse again and write it out, word-for-word in the space provided. There is such value in writing out scripture as it gives you a new view of each word and phrase.

Lockyer points out in his commentary on the psalms that Psalm 121:8 indicates the completeness of God's protection in your life—"God always keeps watch for us in our *going out* to public responsibilities, and the *coming in* to more private affairs." And he goes on to say that "Jehovah has not helped, kept, and blest us all through life to forsake us at the very gate of Heaven. Soulkeeping is the soul of keeping and is an eternal security."[7] Oh what comfort and rest there is in such promises. These are the truths to fix your gaze on in the heat of a trial. Your Lord is right here with you every step of the way.

2. When the psalmist speaks of "your going out" and "your coming in," he is talking about every particular of every day of your life. David speaks of the pilgrimage of our life with the Lord in Psalm 37. Read Psalm 37:23-25 in the selected translations and underline those phrases that mean the most to you today:

> "The steps of a man are established by the LORD, And He delights in his way. When he falls, he will not be hurled headlong, because the LORD is the One who holds his hand. I have been young and now I am old, Yet I have not seen the righteous forsaken or his descendants begging bread" (Psalm 37:23-25 NASB).

> "The LORD directs the steps of the godly. He delights in every detail of their lives. Though they stumble, they will never fall, for the LORD holds them by the hand. Once I was young, and now I am old. Yet I have never seen the godly abandoned or their children begging for bread" (Psalm 37:23-25 NLT).

> "The steps of a good man are ordered by the LORD, and He delights in his way. Though he fall, he shall not be utterly cast down; For the LORD upholds him with His hand. I have been young, and now am old; Yet I have not seen the righteous forsaken, nor his descendants begging bread" (Psalm 37:23-25 NKJV).

3. What hope do you gain today knowing that the Lord is with you every step of the way on into eternity? Write your thoughts in the space provided.

ADORE GOD IN PRAYER

Pray the words of F.B. Meyer today: "I ask, gracious Lord, that you keep me watchful and alert, so that at any moment I may discern the movement of your hand and detect your will and guidance in the providence of little things."[8]

YIELD YOURSELF TO GOD

When we go out in the morning to labour, and come home at eventide to rest, Jehovah shall keep us. When we go out in youth to begin life, and come in at the end to die, we shall experience the same keeping. Our exits and our entrances are under one protection. Three times have we the phrase, "Jehovah shall keep," as if the sacred Trinity thus sealed the word to make it sure: ought not all our fears to be slain by such a threefold flight of arrows? What anxiety can survive this triple promise? This keeping is eternal; continuing from this time forth, even for evermore. The whole church is thus assured of everlasting security: the final perseverance of the saints is thus ensured, and the glorious immortality of believers is guaranteed. Under the aegis of such a promise we may go on pilgrimage without trembling, and venture into battle without dread. None are so safe as those whom God keeps; none so much in danger as the self-secure. To goings out and comings in belong peculiar dangers, since every change of position turns a fresh quarter to the foe, and it is for these Weak points that an especial security is provided: Jehovah will keep the door when it opens and closes, and this he will perseveringly continue to do so long as there is left a single man that trusteth in him, as long as a danger survives, and, in fact, as long as time endures. Glory be unto the Keeper of Israel, who is endeared to us under that title, since our growing sense of weakness makes us feel more deeply than ever our need of being kept. "God keep thee safe from harm and sin, thy spirit keep; the Lord watch o'er thy going out, thy coming in, from this time, evermore.[9]

CHARLES HADDON SPURGEON IN THE TREASURY OF DAVID

ENJOY HIS PRESENCE

We are on our way from earth to heaven and that is a fact never to be forgotten. Someday the temporal façade of a fallen world is going to give way to the eternal and there will be a new heaven and a new earth. The promise is this: "Then I saw a new heaven and a new earth; for the first heaven and the first earth passed away, and there is no longer any sea. And I saw the holy city, new Jerusalem, coming down out of heaven from God, made ready as a bride adorned for her husband. And I heard a loud voice from the throne, saying, Behold, the tabernacle of God is among men, and He will dwell among them, and they shall be His people, and God Himself will be among the, and He will wipe away every tear from their eyes; and there will no longer be any death; there will no longer be any mourning, or crying, or pain; the first things have passed away. And He who sits on the throne said, Behold, I am making all things new" (Revelation 21:1-5). When you are a child of God, you can take great comfort in the fact that your future is secure and your Lord watches over and guards you every step of the way until you see Him face to face. As you close your time with the Lord, how has the Lord met you? How has He been your helper and your keeper and the shade on your right hand? Write your thoughts in the space provided.

REST IN HIS LOVE

"The steps of a man are established by the LORD, and He delights in his way" (Psalm 37:23).

DEVOTIONAL READING
BY HORATIUS BONAR

DEAR FRIEND,

This week you had the opportunity to study Psalm 121 and find hope when you are in need of help. Look over your quiet times from Week Seven. How did God encourage you?

What were your most meaningful discoveries this week as you spent time with the Lord?

Most meaningful insight:

Most meaningful devotional reading:

Most meaningful verse:

A s you think about all that you have learned this week, meditate on these words by Horatius Bonar in *Springs In The Valley* by Mrs. Charles Cowman:

I stand upon the mount of God
With sunlight in my soul;

I hear the storms in vales beneath,
I hear the thunders roll.

But I am calm with thee, my God,
Beneath these glorious skies;
And to the height on which I stand,
No storms, or clouds, can rise.

O, THIS is life! O, this is joy!
My God, to find thee so;
Thy face to see, thy voice to hear,
And all thy love to know.[10]

The Help Of The Lord

In Week Seven of *A Heart That Hopes In God*, we studied Psalm 121, an encouragement for the times when we need help. In this message I want to talk with you about the powerful truths from these eight verses. If you are needing help today, then grab your Bible, these notes, and let's dig in to the amazing Word of God found in Psalm 121.

"I will lift up my eyes to the mountains; from where shall my help come? My help comes from the LORD, who made heaven and earth" (Psalm 121:1-2).

What is the help of the Lord?

The word "help" is *ezer* and means divine aid and assistance, both materially and spiritually.

You have a choice in life. You can be _____-sufficient or

_____-sufficient.

Why is the Lord such an incredible help?

1. He is _____enough. Verse 2

2. He is _____enough. Verse 2

3. He is _____and_____ enough. Verse 3

4. He is _____enough. Verse 4

5. He is _____and_____ enough. Verse 5

6. He is _____and _____ enough. Verse 5

7. He is _____ and _____ enough. Verse 6

8. He is _____enough. Verse 7

9. He is _____ enough. Verse 7

10. He is _____ enough. Verse 8

11. He is _____enough. Verse 8

How can you experience the help of the Lord in your life?

1. _____the promise.

2._____the promise.

3. _____the promise.

4. _____the promise.

Video messages are available on DVDs or as Downloadable M4V Video. Audio messages are available on Audio CDs or as Downloadable MP3 Audio. Visit the Quiet Time Ministries Online Store at www.quiettime.org.

Week Eight

HOPE FOR ALL YOUR NEEDS

Psalm 23

Hope itself is like a star—not to be seen in the sunshine of prosperity, and only to be discovered in the night of adversity. Afflictions are often the black foils in which God doth set the jewels of His children's graces, to make them shine the better.

CHARLES HADDON SPURGEON

WHEN THERE IS NO ONE

The LORD is my shepherd, I shall not want.
PSALM 23:1

PREPARE YOUR HEART

For those who have lived in the Bible for many years, there are favorite passages of Scripture where light has been given in the darkness and joy has been discovered in the sorrow of a rough road in life. Those favorites are different for each child of God as every walk with the Lord is unique and custom-made for that person. However, there are those special diamonds in the setting enjoyed and loved by all. Psalm 23 is one of those places in the Bible that has brought comfort to all who have visited or even made their home there for awhile. Spurgeon called Psalm 23 "the Pearl of Psalms whose soft and pure radiance delights every eye."

Psalm 23 is known as the Shepherd's Psalm and how fitting that it is written by a shepherd about the Great Shepherd. There is no known historical event attached to it in the superscription. Herbert Lockyer believes this was intentional and enables every person to take this psalm to his or her heart.

It is only fitting that we end our journey in the psalms with this highlight in all of Scripture. And while it is always sad to complete one study, there is a joy in knowing that the best is yet to come. We have the incredible blessing to walk with the Lord, always looking forward to the day when we meet Him face to face. Your journey through the Psalms has given you many reasons to hope. As you begin your time with the Lord will you stop and ask the Lord to show you what He has for you in Psalm 23. Ask Him to speak to your heart and give you reason to hope.

READ AND STUDY GOD'S WORD

1. Psalm 23 was written by David who spent years as a shepherd of sheep in preparation to be the King of God's people. Take some time now and read Psalm 23. What is your first impression of this psalm? In what way does it encourage you?

2. Read Psalm 23 again and write out everything you learn about the Lord.

3. There is a time in your life when there is seemingly no one who can be there for you. In fact, it may even seem there is no kindness, no love, no care from any direction. That's the time when you need to know you have a shepherd. Your shepherd is the Lord. That's what Psalm 23:1 is all about—the Lord, your shepherd. We learn in the New Testament that the Lord Jesus is the good shepherd. Look at the following words of Jesus and write everything you learn about Him.

John 10:10-18

John 10:27-30

4. What value is there in having a shepherd? Write your insights in the space provided.

ADORE GOD IN PRAYER

Talk with the Lord today about the fact that He is your Shepherd. Thank Him for being there to meet you in the depth of your own need. Then, lay all your needs out before Him.

YIELD YOURSELF TO GOD

Jehovah is represented successively as the true Shepherd and Guide and Host of his people. And we are taught to think much less of ourselves in our relations with Him, and more of Him as being responsible for us. After all, it is not so much a question of what we are to Jesus, as of what He is to us. The flock does not keep the Shepherd, but the Shepherd the flock. Look away from self, and trust Him to keep and lead and feed. All that we should care for, is not knowingly to resist any of his gracious promptings and teachings…Let God see to your wants. There is nothing you really need for which you may not count on Him.[1]

F.B. MEYER IN CHOICE NOTES ON THE PSALMS

What condescension is this, that the Infinite Lord assumes towards his people the office and character of a Shepherd! It should be the subject of grateful admiration that the great God allows himself to be compared to anything which will set forth his great love and care for his own people. David had himself been a keeper of sheep, and understood both the needs of the sheep and the many cares of a shepherd. He compares himself to a creature weak, defenseless, and foolish, and he takes God to be his Provider, Preserver, Director, and, indeed, his everything.[2]

CHARLES HADDON SPURGEON IN THE TREASURY OF DAVID

Happy the soul that, looking to Jesus as the great, the good, the one Shepherd, can add in truth, And He is mine. I have heard His calling voice; I have seen His inviting smile; I have fled to Him; I have entered into His fold; I have committed myself to His guardian care; He has received me; He has given me most gracious welcome; "I am my Beloved's, and my Beloved is mine."[3]

HENRY LAW IN DAILY PRAYER AND PRAISE

ENJOY HIS PRESENCE

Have you fled to Him and entered His fold? Then you know His most gracious welcome. One of the promises that is yours because the Lord is your Shepherd is that you have everything you need. He is the great I AM, the LORD, whose name means that your God is eternal and beyond the realm of time, has inexhaustible resources, and is all-sufficient. This same God has stooped down to be your Shepherd, always with you twenty four hours a day, to take care of you. That's what a Shepherd does. He cares for you even when no one else does. Are you in need of your Shepherd today? How does knowing the Lord is your Shepherd encourage you and give you hope today? Write your insights in the space provided.

REST IN HIS LOVE

"My sheep hear My voice, and I know them, and they follow Me; and I give eternal life to them, and they will never perish; and no one will snatch them out of My hand" (John 10:27-28).

WHEN YOU ARE TIRED AND WORN OUT

He makes me lie down in green pastures; He leads me beside quiet waters. He restores my soul; He guides me in the paths of righteousness for His name's sake.

PSALM 23:2-3

PREPARE YOUR HEART

The Shepherd knows His sheep better than they know themselves. He knows what they need and when they need it. And He knows when they need to get away and rest awhile. That's the promise of Psalm 23. As you begin your time with the Lord, think about the question, Where are you? It's the question the Lord asked Adam in the garden of Eden and it's a good question as you think about the need for rest and quiet. Do you have such a need today? If so, draw near to the Lord and ask Him to show you what it will mean to lie down in green pastures and be led beside quiet waters. Ask Him to restore your soul and guide you in the paths of righteousness.

READ AND STUDY GOD'S WORD

1. There is such a storehouse of comfort in Psalm 23:2-3. Read these verses in the following translations and underline those phrases that mean the most to you today.

> "He makes me lie down in green pastures; He leads me beside quiet waters. He restores my soul; He guides me in the paths of righteousness for His name's sake." NASB.

> "He makes me lie down in [fresh, tender] green pastures; He leads me beside the still and restful waters. He refreshes and restores my life (my self); He leads me in the paths of righteousness [uprightness and right standing with Him—not for my earning it, but] for His name's sake." AMP

> "He lets me rest in green meadows; he leads me beside peaceful streams. He renews my strength. He guides me along right paths, bringing honor to his name." NLT

"He lets me rest in green pastures. He leads me to calm water. He gives me new strength. He leads me on paths that are right for the good of his name." NCV

2. What is your favorite phrase in these verses and why?

3. Rest and refreshment is biblical. Jesus highly recommends it. Look at the following words of Jesus and write out all that you learn today.

Matthew 11:28-30

Mark 6:30-32

ADORE GOD IN PRAYER

Talk with the Lord today about those areas where you need the place of green pastures, quiet waters, soul and strength restoration, and guidance. Write a prayer to the Lord using the words of Psalm 23 as your guide.

YIELD YOURSELF TO GOD

There are times when grace appears to fade, when trials trouble and depress, when lively vigour faints and deadness chills the soul. Sad indeed would be the issue unless the watchful Shepherd rendered succour; but He assists the downcast; He shows reviving smiles; He brings the cordial of some precious promise. The withering leaf renews its freshness; the tottering limbs again are strong; the heavenward path in ways of righteousness is again stoutly trod.[4]

HENRY LAW IN DAILY PRAYER AND PRAISE

The Christian life has two elements in it, the contemplative and the active, and both of these are richly provided for. First, the contemplative, "He maketh me to lie down in green pastures." What are these "green pastures" but the Scriptures of truth—always fresh, always rich, and never exhausted? There is no fear of biting the bare ground where the grass is long enough for the flock to lie down in it. Sweet and full are the doctrines of the gospel; fit food for souls, as tender grass is natural nutriment for sheep. When by faith we are enabled to find rest in the promises, we are like the sheep that lie down in the midst of the pasture; we find at the same moment both provender and peace, rest and refreshment, serenity and satisfaction. But observe: "He maketh me to lie down." It is the Lord who graciously enables us to perceive the preciousness of his truth, and to feed upon it. How grateful ought we to be for the power to appropriate the promises! There are some distracted souls who would give worlds if they could but do this. They know the blessedness of it, but they cannot say that this blessedness is theirs. They know the "green pastures," but they are not made to "lie down" in them. Those believers who have for years enjoyed a "full assurance of faith" should greatly bless their gracious God. The second part of a vigorous Christian's life consists in gracious activity. We not only think, but we act. We are not always lying down to feed, but are journeying onward toward perfection; hence we read, "He leadeth me beside the still waters." What are these "still waters" but the influences and graces of his blessed Spirit? His Spirit attends us in various operations, like waters—in the plural to cleanse, to refresh, to fertilize, to cherish.[5]

CHARLES HADDON SPURGEON IN THE TREASURY OF DAVID

ENJOY HIS PRESENCE

Have you discovered the rich green pastures of the Word of God? No wonder Jeremiah said, "Your words were found and I ate them, and Your words became for me a joy and the delight of my heart; For I have been called by Your name, O LORD God of hosts" (Jeremiah 15:16). Do you take time to be still and know that He is God? Close your time with the Lord by writing a prayer, expressing all that is on your heart.

REST IN HIS LOVE

"Come away with Me by yourselves to a quiet place and rest a little while" (Mark 6:31 wms).

WHEN YOU FACE THE SHADOW OF DEATH

Even though I walk through the valley of the shadow of death, I fear no evil, for You are with me; Your rod and Your staff, they comfort me.

Psalm 23:4

PREPARE YOUR HEART

There is no road on our journey that has not been traveled by Jesus, our Savior. Never is this more true than in the "valley of the shadow of death." There came a day when He cried out to God His Father, "Father, Into Your hands I commit My spirit" (Luke 23:46). The following words tell us that "Having said this, He breathed His last." Something happened three days later that changed everything—Jesus rose from the dead. What He accomplished impacts our experience with the valley of the shadow of death. Here is the great encouragement: "Behold, I tell you a mystery; we will not all sleep, but we will all be changed, in a moment, in the twinkling of an eye, at the last trumpet; for the trumpet will sound, and the dead will be raised imperishable, and we will be changed. For this perishable must put on the imperishable, and this mortal must put on immortality. But when this perishable will have put on the imperishable, and this mortal will have put on immortality, then will come about the saying that is written, 'DEATH IS SWALLOWED UP in victory. O DEATH, WHERE IS YOUR VICTORY? O DEATH, WHERE IS YOUR STING?' The sting of death is sin, and the power of sin is the law; but thanks be to God, who gives us the victory through our Lord Jesus Christ" (1 Corinthians 15:51-57).

Oh what promises are yours in the face of the valley of the shadow of death! Paul says, "For now we in a mirror dimly, but then face to face; now I know in part, but then I will know fully just as I also have been fully known" (1 Corinthians 13:12). Face to face and complete knowledge are promises for the experience of heaven when we step into eternity. Paul also encourages us that the preference for all of us is "to be absent from the body and to be at home with the Lord" (2 Corinthians 5:8).

Corrie ten Boom used to always say, "Jesus is Victor." And that stands true even in the valley of the shadow of death. According to Paul, nothing, not even death, can separate us from the love of God, which is in Christ Jesus our Lord (Romans 8:38-39). As you contemplate these powerful truths, ask God to quiet your heart and speak to you today.

READ AND STUDY GOD'S WORD

1. Read Psalm 23:4 and write out the reasons why there is no fear of harm or evil in the valley of the shadow of death.

2. There are four powerful words in this verse that take all the fear out of anything you face: "You are with me." Just think—you are able to say "Lord, You are with me no matter what I go through, even death." What does it mean to you to know that the Lord is with you today?

3. The rod and the staff bring comfort to the psalmist and they can bring comfort to you as well. They are representative of the Shepherd's care because they are used to drive away any threat and provide strength that sustains you. These are not words only for one who faces death but for one who faces any kind of adversity. The shepherd is able to protect the sheep in times of danger. Keller points out that the sheep pass through valleys from the lowlands to the highlands. The valleys offer rich pasture and water, but are also places of danger from storms and wild animals. There are shadows in the valley because of the lack of sunlight. James Montgomery Boice points out that the shadows are as much a part of God's path for us as the green pastures and quiet waters. Life is not always tranquil. There are valleys and often it is in the valley where the making of a man or woman of God occurs. And so, it is necessary to surrender to the Lord in the valley and

allow Him to lead you. But take courage, the rod and the staff are always there administering His tender care all along the way.

4. Read the following verses and record what you learn about the care of the Lord:

Mark 4:35-41

2 Corinthians 1:3-5

1 Peter 5:7

ADORE GOD IN PRAYER

Pray the words of F.B. Meyer today: "For those I love, for all who are in sickness and sorrow, for those who anticipate this day with anxiety; for those who are called to suffer, to undergo special trials, to pass through the valley of the shadow, I humbly pray that they may be provided as they need."[6]

YIELD YOURSELF TO GOD

Our sorest trial is when, with feeble step, we traverse the cheerless vale of death. The climate is chilly. Nature fails. We shrink from the icy hand; but still there is no fear. The tender Shepherd is by our side: His gentle guidance removes apprehension. The waters fail to overwhelm. Sweet texts bring light, and the Spirit applies comfort...To lean on Jesus in the darkest hour is light and joy and peace. The Good Shepherd knows the chilly hand of death. He has passed this darksome vale; but His God was with Him. Ministering angels brought support. He found no evil, and no evil shall destroy His sheep.[7]

HENRY LAW IN DAILY PRAYER AND PRAISE

ENJOY HIS PRESENCE

What have you learned today from your quiet time that gives you hope? Articulate your thoughts in the space provided and then carry what you have learned with you throughout the day.

REST IN HIS LOVE

"…casting all your anxiety on Him, because He cares for you" (1 Peter 5:7).

WHEN YOUR ENEMY COMES AGAINST YOU

*You prepare a table before me in the presence of my enemies; You
have anointed my head with oil; my cup overflows.*

PSALM 23:5

PREPARE YOUR HEART

The greatest need for hope is when your enemy attacks you. Whether you realize it or not, there is a spiritual battle taking place. And you have an enemy who would love to defeat you. The enemy loves to attack when you are in a time of trouble. Peter tells us, "Be of sober spirit, be on the alert. Your adversary, the devil, prowls around like a roaring lion, seeking someone to devour. But resist him, firm in your faith, knowing that the same experiences of suffering are being accomplished by your brethren who are in the world. After you have suffered for a little while, the God of all grace, who called you to His eternal glory in Christ, will Himself perfect, confirm, strengthen and establish you" (1 Peter 5:8-10). You can have great courage in the spiritual battle. The Bible promises, "…greater is He who is in you than he who is in the world." You see, Psalm 23:5 tells us something important that we can know in the face of an attack by the enemy. The Lord prepares a table before you in the presence of your enemy. And the anointing of the Holy Spirit as He controls and empowers you when you are filled with the Holy Spirit will give you an overflowing life. These are the promises of Psalm 23:5. Ask the Lord to open your eyes today to these promises that give you hope.

READ AND STUDY GOD'S WORD

1. Read Psalm 23:5 in the following translations and underline your favorite phrases in each one.

> "You prepare a table before me in the presence of my enemies; You have anointed my head with oil; my cup overflows." NASB

"You prepare a feast for me in the presence of my enemies. You welcome me as a guest, anointing my head with oil. My cup overflows with blessings." NLT

"You treat me to a feast, while my enemies watch. You honor me as your guest, and you fill my cup until it overflows." CEV

2. Take a moment to think about that statement, "You prepare a table before me in the presence of my enemies." What you want to do is meditate on this verse, live in it for a moment and think about what it means. To do this means to ask some questions about it and answer those questions with truth from the Word of God. So let's go deeper into this verse and think about what God is saying here. Your enemy has attacked. What is the Lord promising He will do when the enemy attacks? He will prepare a "table." The other translations point out the presence of a feast. Imagine in your own mind a table laden with all kinds of food. There is a question in Psalm 78:19, "Can God prepare a table in the wilderness?" And we know the answer is "yes." God answered that question when He fed the people of Israel for forty years as they wandered in the wilderness. And He has answered the question here in Psalm 23:5 through David as we see that He prepares a table where we can feast during the attack of an enemy. And we see the table again in Revelation 3:20 in the words of Jesus, "Behold, I stand at the door and knock; if anyone hears My voice and opens the door, I will come in to him and will dine with him, and he with Me." We also know through the testimony of Jeremiah that there is a feast waiting in the Word of God, "Your words were found and I ate them, and Your words became for me a joy and the delight of my heart" (Jeremiah 15:16). And so, when your enemy attacks, run to the Word of God, sit with your Lord, and eat and drink in all that He says. The Word of God is your offensive weapon in spiritual warfare and you will gain new strength as you live in it daily: "And take THE HELMET OF SALVATION, and the sword of the Spirit, which is the word of God" (Ephesians 6:17).

And that leads to your other strength in spiritual warfare revealed in Psalm 23:5: the Holy Spirit. You need the power of the Holy Spirit. The word in Psalm 23:5 is "anointed" and the psalmist speaks of an anointing with oil. Boice points out in his commentary that oil was necessary in the dry, barren lands of the Near East. There is a dry, barren land in the heart particularly evident in spiritual warfare. That dry barren heart is desperately in need of the rivers of living water that come from the Holy Spirit. Jesus said, "If anyone is thirsty, let him come to Me and drink. He who believes in Me, as the Scripture said, 'From his innermost being will flow rivers of living water.' But this He spoke of the Spirit whom those who believed in Him were to receive..." (John 7:37-39). The Holy Spirit is that anointing we receive from Jesus spoken of in 1 John 2:27, "As for you, the anointing which you received from Him abides in you..." We need the power of the Holy Spirit every day of our lives. Paul encourages us to be filled (controlled and empowered) by the Holy Spirit. "And do not get drunk with wine, for that is dissipation, but be filled with the Spirit" (Ephesians 5:18). F.B. Meyer says, "We must be prepared to break through a ring of enemies to feed, and to get the daily anointing of the Holy Spirit."[8] How can we be filled (controlled and empowered) with the Holy Spirit? Confess all known sin in your life and ask the Lord to fill you with His Holy Spirit. You can know that "This is the confidence which we have before Him, that, if we ask anything according to His will, He hears us. And if we know that He hears us in whatever we ask, we know that we have the requests which we have asked from Him." It's God's will that you walk daily in the power of the Holy Spirit. Spiritual battles are not yours to fight—they're His to fight—but you must allow Him to fight the battle and the way you do that is to pray to be filled with His Spirit. Always remember, Jesus is Victor and He is stronger than any enemy you will ever face.

Describe in your own words what it means to you today to have a "table in the wilderness" (see Psalm 23:5 and Psalm 78:19).

3. There is a very powerful passage of Scripture teaching about spiritual warfare. We need to be aware of it and know and understand what it says. Read Ephesians 6:10-18 and record everything you learn about spiritual warfare.

ADORE GOD IN PRAYER

Draw near to the Lord now and confess any known sin He reveals to you. "If we confess our sins, He is faithful and righteous to forgive us our sins and to cleanse us from all unrighteousness" (1 John 1:9). Then, ask the Lord to fill you with His Holy Spirit, to give you His strength and power in the heat of the battle, and to bring you to the table of His Word and allow you to feast there.

YIELD YOURSELF TO GOD

> Our enemies stand round in vast array, but they cannot destroy enjoyments. In their sight God spreads a banquet of delights. His inward unctions (things that serve to soothe) cause the heart to show all kinds of radiant joy, as the countenance refreshed with unguents (soothing ointments). We hold a cup: God's hand supplies it: He pours in pleasures to the extent of capacity to receive. The overjoyed believer feels, "Stay, stay; it is enough;" but still the goblet overflows. Who can measure the delights of God's presence, smile, and word?[9]
>
> HENRY LAW IN DAILY PRAYER AND PRAISE

ENJOY HIS PRESENCE

What have you learned today that will give you hope in the face of an enemy attack?

REST IN HIS LOVE

"Finally, be strong in the Lord and in the strength of His might" (Ephesians 6:10).

HOPE'S BRIGHT CONCLUSION

Surely goodness and lovingkindness will follow me all the days of my life, and I will dwell in the house of the LORD forever.
PSALM 23:6

PREPARE YOUR HEART

Hope comes to a bright conclusion, something you can hold on to no matter what happens in your life. It is "the rest of the story" that counts for you in the end. At the end of the day this is what is true, honorable, right, pure, lovely, good repute, excellent, and worthy of praise (Philippians 4:8). This is the great conclusion, the reality, the truth that you can count on: "Surely goodness and lovingkindness will follow me all the days of my life, and I will dwell in the house of the LORD forever" (Psalm 23:6). How can you come to such a wonderful conclusion? Because God is good and nothing that happens in your life can ever change Who He is. His plans and purposes will come to pass. If you have surrendered your life to Him and received Him as your Savior and Lord, then your eternal future with Him face to face is assured. "And the testimony is this, that God has given us eternal life, and this life is in His Son. He who has the Son has the life; he who does not have the Son of God does not have the life. These things I have written to you who believe in the name of the Son of God, so that you may know that you have eternal life" (1 John 5:11-13). You can joyfully say with the psalmist, "I will dwell in the house of the LORD forever" (Psalm 23:6). Eternity with Him is guaranteed for you. Ask the Lord now to open your eyes to see the wonder of hope's bright conclusion: *eternal life.*

READ AND STUDY GOD'S WORD

1. Read Psalm 23:6 and write it out word-for-word in the space provided.

2. Did you know that heaven and eternal life with your Lord is your great prize in life? Oh what a day it will be for you to meet Him face to face. Look at the following verses and write what you learn about eternal life with the Lord.

John 14:1-3

Revelation 21:1-4

Revelation 22:1-5

3. Take a few moments and look through your quiet times over the last eight weeks. What are the most important truths you have learned that give you hope for your life? Write them out in the space provided.

Adore God in Prayer

Thank the Lord today for all that you have learned in your study in the Psalms. Write a prayer in your journal expressing all that is on your heart today.

Yield Yourself to God

Surely goodness and mercy shall follow me all the days of my life. This is a fact as indisputable as it is encouraging, and therefore a heavenly *verily*, or *surely* is set as a seal upon it. This sentence may be read, "*only* goodness and mercy," for there shall be unmingled mercy in our history. These twin guardian angels will always be with me at my back and my beck. Just as when great princes go abroad they must not go unattended, so it is with the believer. Goodness and mercy follow him always—"*all the days of his life*"—the black days as well as the bright days, the days of fasting as well as the days of feasting, the dreary days of winter as well as the bright days of summer. Goodness supplies our needs, and mercy blots out our sins. "*And I will dwell in the house of the Lord for ever.*" "A servant abideth not in the house for ever, but the son abideth ever." While I am here I will be a child at home with my God; the whole world shall be his house to me; and when I ascend into the upper chamber I shall not change my company, nor even change the house; I shall only go to dwell in the upper storey of the house of the Lord for ever. May God grant us grace to dwell in the serene atmosphere of this most blessed Psalm![10]

CHARLES HADDON SPURGEON IN THE TREASURY OF DAVID

ENJOY HIS PRESENCE

What a treasure there is in the psalms. You have journeyed through some of the choice psalms in the Bible. There are more beauties to be explored in the landscape of the Word of God. Don't allow even one place in all your Bible to remain buried and unknown to you. Instead, resolve to live in every corner of God's Word. What will it take to dare such a venture? Set aside time each day, choose a quiet place, and plan to open the Word of God and sit alone with your Lord. For detailed help in your quiet time, read *Six Secrets To A Powerful Quiet Time*.[11] For more quiet times from A Quiet Time Experience series, choose *Run Before the Wind, Trusting in the Names of God,* and *Passionate Prayer*. Or, you may choose one of the books of quiet times in the Quiet Times For The Heart series: *Pilgrimage Of The Heart, Revive My Heart, A Heart That Dances, A Heart On Fire*, and *A Heart To See Forever*.[12] Dear friend, this is not an end, only a very exciting beginning to the great adventure. And so, God bless you as you continue on in this great adventure of knowing Him!

In the Introduction you wrote a letter to the Lord. Take some time now to read your letter to the Lord written as you began this quiet time experience in the Psalms. How has God answered your prayer and met you in the Psalms?

Close by writing a new letter, a prayer of thanksgiving to your Lord.

REST IN HIS LOVE

"There will no longer be any curse; and the throne of God and of the Lamb will be in it, and His bond-servants will serve Him; they will see His face, and His name will be on their foreheads. And there will no longer be any night; and they will not have need of the light of a lamp nor the light of the sun, because the Lord God will illumine them; and they will reign forever and ever" (Revelation 22:3-5).

DEVOTIONAL READING
BY JOHN HENRY JOWETT

DEAR FRIEND,

In your quiet times this week you have lived in Psalm 23 and discovered how God gives us hope for all our needs. Write a prayer to the Lord expressing all that is on your heart as a result of your time in God's Word in Week Eight.

What were your most meaningful discoveries this week as you spent time with the Lord?

Most meaningful insight:

Most meaningful devotional reading:

Most meaningful verse:

As you think about all that you have learned this week, meditate on these words by John Henry Jowett in *The Silver Lining*: "He hath begotten us again unto a living hope…He that believeth on Me shall never die. What a hope He kindles! Such a hope gives to life an amazing expectancy. When Samuel Rutherford was near his end, he was so gloriously excited at the prospect that those about him had to counsel him to moderate his ecstasy! The fine flavour of that glorious expectancy should pervade all our days. That we are to live forever with the Lord is a prospect that should fill our life with quiet and fruitful amazement. To have that life in front of us will enable us to set all things in true perspective and to observe their true proportions. Set money in the line and light of immortality, and we at once observe the limits of its ministry and range. Set rectitude (moral uprightness) in the same radiant line, and we see how it clothes itself with abounding glory. Everything must be placed in that long and glorious line or nothing will be truly seen. These, then, are some of the hopes kindled and inspired by Jesus Christ our Lord. What He kindles He will keep burning."[13]

Viewer Guide

◈ WEEK EIGHT ◈

The Comfort Of The Lord

It's hard to believe that we have completed our last week of study in *A Heart That Hopes In God.* And it is fitting that we lived in Psalm 23, the blessed comfort for all who face difficult times and fiery trials. Whenever you need hope, you will find precious promises to soothe your soul. In this message, I want to share the comforting hope of Psalm 23.

"The LORD is my shepherd, I shall not want. He makes me lie down in great pastures; He leads me beside quiet waters. He restores my soul" (Psalm 23:1-3).

A. *The Picture of Comfort*

Comfort is all about _____and
_____.

Comfort is a consolation bringing _____and
_____.

The picture is a _____with a shepherd in a green pasture.

B. *The Person of Comfort*—It is the_____.

2 Corinthians 1:3

He knows and cares about my deepest _____.

C. *The God of all comfort has a promise for you*—the promise of _____.

The comfort of God thrives in _____.

2 Corinthians 1:4

D. *How does God provide for your comfort?*

1. He is the God of _____comfort. 2 Corinthians 1:3

2. Jesus gives you _____comfort. 2 Corinthians 1:5

3. The Lord has given you _____Comforter, the Holy Spirit.

John 14:16

4. The Bible _____to our comfort. Romans 15:4

E. *What is the power of comfort?*

Comfort is your _____, giving your soul courage
to hope—holding on with patient expectation.

F. What is the product of comfort?

Comfort _____your hope and helps you keep on
running your race. Acts 9:31

≫ Video messages are available on DVDs or as Downloadable M4V Video. Audio messages
are available on Audio CDs or as Downloadable MP3 Audio. Visit the Quiet Time Ministries Online
Store at www.quiettime.org.

NOW THAT YOU HAVE COMPLETED THESE QUIET TIMES

You have spent eight weeks consistently drawing near to God in quiet time with Him. That time alone with Him does not need to come to an end. What is the next step? To continue your pursuit of God, you might consider other books from the A Quiet Time Experience series, including *Run Before the Wind, Trusting in the Names of God,* and *Passionate Prayer.* The Quiet Times For The Heart series are also books of quiet times with titles such as *Pilgrimage of the Heart, Revive My Heart, A Heart that Dances, A Heart on Fire,* and *A Heart to See Forever..* To learn more about quiet time, read signature books from the A 30-Day Journey series such as *Six Secrets to a Powerful Quiet Time* and *Knowing and Loving the Bible.* Leader's Kits with DVD messages and Leader's Guides are available for each book. Learn more about quiet time from Catherine's many books, *Enriching Your Quiet Time* quarterly magazine, and The Quiet Time Notebook™. Quiet Time Ministries Online has many resources to encourage you in your quiet time with God. Find daily encouragement from Cath's Blog and view A Walk In Grace™, the devotional photojournal featuring Catherine's own photography at www.quiettime.org. Join hundreds of other women online to study God's Word and grow in God's grace at Ministry For Women (www.ministryfor-women.com). Resources may be ordered online from Quiet Time Ministries at www.quiettime. org or by calling Quiet Time Ministries. For more information, you may contact:

Quiet Time Ministries
P.O. Box 14007
Palm Desert, California 92255
(800) 925-6458, (760) 772-2357
E-mail: catherine@quiettime.org
Website: www.quiettime.org

ABOUT THE AUTHOR

Catherine Martin is a summa cum laude graduate of Bethel Theological Seminary with a Master of Arts degree in Theological Studies. She is founder and president of Quiet Time Ministries, director of women's ministries at Southwest Community Church in Indian Wells, California, and adjunct faculty member of Biola University. She is the author of *Six Secrets to a Powerful Quiet Time, Knowing and Loving the Bible, Walking with the God Who Cares, Set my Heart on Fire, Trusting in the Names of God, Passionate Prayer, Quiet Time Moments for Women,* and *Drawing Strength from the Names of God* published by Harvest House Publishers, and *Pilgrimage of the Heart, Revive My Heart!* and *A Heart That Dances,* published by NavPress. She has also written The Quiet Time Notebook™, *A Heart on Fire, A Heart to See Forever,* and *A Heart That Hopes in God,* published by Quiet Time Ministries. She is senior editor for *Enriching Your Quiet Time* quarterly magazine. As a popular speaker at retreats and conferences, Catherine challenges others to seek God and love Him with all of their heart, soul, mind, and strength. For more information about Catherine, visit www.quiettime.org and www.ministryforwomen.com

ABOUT QUIET TIME MINISTRIES

Quiet Time Ministries is a nonprofit religious organization under Section 501(c)(3) of the Internal Revenue Code. Cash donations are tax deductible as charitable contributions. We count on prayerful donors like you, partners with Quiet Time Ministries pursuing our goals of the furtherance of the Gospel of Jesus Christ and teaching devotion to God and His Word. Visit us online at www.quiettime.org to view special funding opportunities and current ministry projects. Your prayerful donations bring countless project to life!

Quiet Time Ministries | P.O. Box 14007 | Palm Desert, California 92255
1.800.925.6458 | catherine@quiettime.org | www.quiettime.org | www.ministryforwomen.com

APPENDIX

DISCUSSION QUESTIONS

Introduction

Begin your class with prayer and then welcome everyone to this new book of quiet times. Have the people in your group share their names and what brought them to the study. Make sure each person in your group has a book. Also, gather contact information for all participants in your group including name, address, phone number, and e-mail. That way you can keep in touch and encourage those in your group.

Familiarize your group with the layout of the book. Each week consists of five days of quiet times, as well as a devotional reading and response for days 6 and 7. Each day follows the PRAYER quiet time plan:

Prepare Your Heart

Read and Study God's Word

Adore God in Prayer

Yield Yourself to God

Enjoy His Presence

Rest in His Love

Journal and prayer pages are included in the back of the book. Note that the quiet times offer devotional reading, Bible study, prayer, and practical application. Some days are longer than others and therefore, they should study at their own pace. Days 6-7 are for catching up, review, etc. This is a concentrated, intentional journey on hope in the Psalms. Encourage your group to interact with the study, underlining significant insights and writing comments in the margins. Encourage your group to read the Introduction sometime the first day. Also point out that the Introduction includes a place where they will write a letter to the Lord. Encourage them to draw near to God each day and ask Him to speak to their hearts.

You can determine how to organize your group sessions, but here's one idea: Discuss the week of quiet times together in the first hour, break for ten minutes, and then watch the message on the companion DVD. There are nine messages for *A Heart That Hopes In God*—one for the introduction and one for each week. You might also share with your group a summary of how to prepare for their quiet time by setting aside a time each day and a place. Consider sharing how time alone with the Lord has made a difference in your own life. Let your class know about the Quiet Time Ministries website at www.quiettime.org and also Ministry For Women at www. ministryforwomen.com.

Another option is to divide each week (completing the study in 16 weeks) by discussing days 1–3 one week and days 4–7 another week. This allows your group to journey through each quiet time at a slower pace.

Pray for one another by offering a way to record and exchange prayer requests. Some groups like to pass around a basket with cards that people can use to record prayer requests. Then, people take a request out of the basket and pray for someone during the week. Others like to use three by five cards and then exchange cards on a weekly basis.

Close this introductory class with prayer, take a short break, and then show the companion DVD message.

Week One: There is Always Hope No Matter What

This week, the goal of your discussion is to understand what hope is and how you can have hope no matter what you experience in life. This study is such an encouragement for anyone who is going through a difficult time. You will have wonderful discussions that will help your group stand strong in the storms of life. You want your group to be able to define hope and to realize that hope is always possible because of God and His Word.

This week is an overview of a heart that hopes in God. You might introduce your discussion by sharing that in this first week, your group had the opportunity to look at the certainty of hope, the definition of hope, how to have hope, the nature of hope, and the benefit of hope. In the weeks to come, we will be looking at specific psalms that help us experience the hope of the Lord.

DAY 1: The Certainty of Hope

You might begin this first week of discussion with a brief overview of what they studied. You might say something like: *This week we are looking at how we can have hope no matter what we face in life.*

1. Open your discussion with prayer. Ask any new members of your group to introduce themselves. Share the goal of these quiet times: to learn about how to have a heart that hopes in God.

2. You began by reading the great promise in Romans 15:13. What was your favorite phrase in this verse and why?

3. What was your favorite insight from the devotional thoughts of Spurgeon?

DAY 2: The Definition of Hope

1. What is hope?

2. What is the difference between God's kind of hope and the hope that you see in the world?

3. Why do we sometimes "lose hope" in life and fall into despair?

4. What will encourage us to never lose hope?

DAY 3: The Way to Hope

1. According to Romans 15:4, how can we have hope?

2. What did you learn about God's Word?

3. Why does it take a decision on our part to be in the Bible, God's Word each day?

DAY 4: The Nature of Hope

1. What meant the most to you as you looked at the lives of Horatio Spafford, Job, Jeremiah, and Paul?

2. What did you learn from the writing of Spurgeon in Day 4?

DAY 5: The Benefit of Hope

1. Why is an "anchor for your soul" such a good picture for "hope?" Why do we need an anchor for our soul?

2. How can you tell that a person has the kind of hope that God gives?

DAYS 6 AND 7: Devotional Reading by Charles Haddon Spurgeon

1. What was your favorite verse, insight, or quote from your quiet times this week?

2. What did you learn from the excerpt written by Charles Haddon Spurgeon in Day 6 and 7?

3. What is the most important truth you learned about hope? How can you apply it in your own life? Close your time together in prayer.

Week Two: Hope When You Feel Alone

The goal this week is to discover the great promises in Psalm 139 and find hope when you feel alone. You might begin by reviewing with your group what they learned last week about hope. Emphasize the difference between wishing, wanting, and God's kind of hope that is a certainty based on fact. Share the acrostic H.O.P.E.—Holding On with Patient Expectation.

DAY 1: He Knows Me

1. Open your discussion with prayer. Then share that this week you had the opportunity to live in Psalm 139 written by David, the man after God's own heart. And you discovered that there is great hope when you feel alone in life.

2. Begin by asking "how were you encouraged by your time alone with the Lord this week?"

3. What did you think about Psalm 139 and how did it give you hope this week?

4. In Day 1, you looked at the fact that God knows you. What was your favorite part of Psalm 139:1-6?

5. What did you learn from the meeting of Jesus and Nathaniel?

6. How were you encouraged in your own relationship with the Lord as you read the verses and devotional reading?

DAY 2: He is With Me

1. You began your quiet time in Day 2 by reading a prayer from *The Valley Of Vision*. What was your favorite part of that prayer and why?

2. In Day 2 you looked at the truth that God is with you. What was most significant to you from Psalm 139:7-12?

3. What did you learn in the reading from The Pursuit Of God by A.W. Tozer?

DAY 3: He Created Me

1. In Day 3 you thought about the truth that God created you. How did the story of Ponnamal impact you?

2. What does it mean for you to know that God made you, dreamed of you, and desired you for His very own? How does that give you hope?

DAY 4: He Has a Plan for Me

1. In Day 4 you looked at the truth that God has a plan for you. Sometimes in the living out of that plan we experience the loss of a dream. What did you learn about that in your time with the Lord?

2. Have you ever experienced the death of a dream and what did you learn from the Lord? How did you see the working out of God's plan?

3. What was your most significant insight from your time with the Lord in Day 4?

DAY 5: He Thinks About Me

1. In Day 5 you saw that the Lord thinks about you. As you thought about this truth, what impacted you the most?

2. What was most significant to you as you meditated on the verses about God's love?

DAYS 6 AND 7: Devotional Reading by Amy Carmichael

1. What was your favorite verse, insight, or quote from your quiet times this week?

2. What did you learn from the excerpt by Amy Carmichael in Days 6-7?

3. What is the most important truth you learned about God this week? How can you apply it in your own life and how will it bring you hope? Then, close in prayer.

Week Three: Hope When You are in Trouble

DAY 1: The Fiery Trial

You might begin your discussion by reviewing what the class discussed the last two weeks about hope including the definition of H.O.P.E.—Holding On with Patient Expectation. Share briefly about all you learned from Psalm 139 and the character of God – that He knows, He is with you, He created you, He has a plan for you, and He thinks about you. Your goal for your discussion today is to help your group understand the promises in Psalm 31 that will give them hope when they are in trouble.

1. Open your discussion with prayer. Give a brief review of what they've learned in the last two weeks of study. Then you might begin by sharing that this week we want to look at how we can have hope when we are in trouble. And to do that we are going to look at Psalm 31.

2. We began our quiet time experience this week by looking at the example of Annie Johnson Flint. What did you learn from her example and how did she demonstrate her own hope in the Lord?

3. Who was Psalm 31 written by and what was his trial? Why did he need hope?

4. When you initially read Psalm 31, what stood out to you at first about this psalm?

5. Why is it so difficult to have hope in a trial?

DAY 2: Anatomy of a Trial

1. Describe what makes a trial really a trial.

2. What is the most difficult part of a trial for you?

3. What promise from Psalm 31 brings the most hope for you right now?

4. What was your favorite part of William Cowper's poem in *Yield Yourself To God*?

DAY 3: An Alternate View of the Trial

1. When you think about the suffering that others face, why is it that some seem to be able to persevere and others just give up? What makes the difference according to your study in Day 3?

2. Look at the truths about trials in *Prepare Your Heart* on Day 3. What can you know about your trial? Have different people share what the Bible has to say about trials.

3. Psalm 31 is a psalm filled with hope. What truths and promises gave David hope according to Psalm 31? What did he know to be true about God?

4. What's your favorite truth that gives you hope from Psalm 31?

5. What did you learn from Octavius Winslow in *Help Heavenward*?

DAY 4: The Secret Place in the Trial

1. In Day 4 you learned that there is a secret place in a trial? Where is the secret place in a trial? What does that phrase actually mean?

2. What did you learn about the Lord as your shelter and your secret place?

3. How can you experience the "secret place" of His Presence?

4. What was your favorite quote from today's reading?

DAY 5: His Marvelous Lovingkindness in the Trial

1. Have someone in the class read Psalm 31:21.

2. We see that David's trouble enabled him to experience God's lovingkindness in new ways. But the trials of David required a certain response. From Psalm 31 what do you see in David's life—how did he respond in the trials?

3. What did you learn about prayer from the example of David? What was your favorite prayer?

4. What did you learn from Annie Johnson Flint's poem in *Yield Yourself To God*?

5. What has the Lord taught you in the trials in your own life?

6. How have you experienced God's love in the midst of a trial?

DAYS 6 AND 7: Devotional Reading by Octavius Winslow

1. In Days Six and Seven you had the opportunity to read from Octavius Winslow. What was your favorite truth from his writing?

2. You closed your week by writing a prayer to the Lord. Would some in the group be willing to read all or part of their prayer?

3. Close your time by praying Peter Marshall's prayer in Adore God In Prayer from Day 4.

Week Four: Hope When You are Discouraged

The goal for your discussion is to lead your group to a deeper understanding of how they can have hope when they are discouraged. You want you group to learn from the great example of David, the man after God's own heart, in Psalm 18.

DAY 1: Who Do I Love?

1. Open your discussion with prayer. Share briefly about your discussion last week about how to have hope when you are in trouble. We saw that David, who was the author of Psalm 31, knew what it was to be in trouble. And yet, he knew how to run to God and find shelter in the secret place of His Presence. The result is that David experienced the love of God in the midst of the trial. He spoke of his experience this way: "He has made marvelous His lovingkindness to me in a besieged city" (Psalm 31:21). Now, this week, we have spent time with David in another of his psalms, Psalm 18. This psalm will give you hope when you are discouraged. You might begin by asking, "Why do you think at times we become discouraged in life?"

2. One of the examples you read about this week was G. Campbell Morgan. Describe how he became discouraged and what happened to change him during this time.

3. You had the opportunity to begin your week of quiet times by reading Psalm 18 and giving it a title. Let's share some of our titles (if you have a whiteboard as a visual aid, you may even want to write the different titles out as others share).

4. Ask those in your group to describe David's relationship with God. What was it like?

5. What was your favorite part of the reading from *Streams in the Desert* by Mrs. Charles Cowman?

6. What is the first thing we should do when are discouraged?

DAY 2: Who Do I Call?

1. Have someone in the group read Psalm 18:3. Ask your class what you learn here about what to do in a time of discouragement.

2. How does prayer help you when you are discouraged?

3. What did you learn about prayer and God's response in the verses you studied?

4. What did you learn from the quotes you read?

5. Can you think of a time when you were discouraged and prayer helped you?

DAY 3: What Will God Do?

1. Psalm 18 is filled with truths about who God is and what He does. As you spent time with this psalm writing out all these truths, what did you learn about God?

2. As you read through this psalm and saw the words of David in much greater detail, what did you discover about David's relationship with the Lord?

3. What was your favorite truth about God this week and why did it mean so much to you?

DAY 4: What Will I Learn about God?

1. In Day Four you began thinking more deeply about the character of God and the whole idea of "praise in advance." What was your favorite phrase or sentence in the quote by Spurgeon in *Prepare Your Heart*?

2. You looked at what David said about God in Psalm 18:28-36. What phrases did you underline in that section of the psalm?

3. What was most significant to you about God and why did it mean so much to you?

4. What were your favorite insights from Spurgeon's *Treasury of David*, his commentary on the Psalms?

5. You also had the opportunity to write out all the prayer requests you have right now. What are your greatest prayer needs right now that you could share with the group? (you might ask your group to use one of the prayer pages to record the requests of others so they can pray for each other over the next week).

DAY 5: What Will I Do?

1. In Day Five you learned more about the value of praise and thanksgiving. Have someone read Psalm 18:49 as you discuss what you learned from this day.

2. What is the value of praise and thanksgiving in a time of discouragement?

3. What did David resolve to do in Psalm 18:49?

4. What did you learn about thanksgiving and praise from the verses you looked at in the New Testament?

5. Why is it difficult to praise and thank the Lord in a time of discouragement and what do you think enables us to have a heart of praise in those times?

6. Can you think of a time when you were able to thank the Lord in the midst of a trial?

7. What were you able to thank God for this week?

DAYS 6 AND 7: Devotional Reading by James Montgomery Boice

1. In days 6 and 7 you had the opportunity to read from James Montgomery Boice. What was your favorite truth from his writing?

2. Did you have a favorite quote, insight, or verse?

3. To summarize, what is the one thing that will give you hope when you are discouraged—it may be a truth about God or something that you learned from the example of David?

4. Close in prayer.

Week Five: Hope When You Need Deliverance

Your goal in your discussion this week is to help those in your group understand the promises from Psalm 34 that will give them hope when they need deliverance in a trial or difficulty.

DAY 1: The God of Deliverances

1. Open your discussion with prayer. Share briefly about your discussion last week about how to have hope when you are discouraged. We saw that David, who was the author of Psalm 31, knew what it was to be discouraged. Psalm 18 shows that he loved the Lord, he called out to the Lord, and God rescued him, Now, this week, we have spent time with David in another of his psalms, Psalm 34. This psalm will give you hope when you need a deliverance. And we discovered that God is the God of deliverances. Have someone in your group read Psalm 34:4. As we begin our time of discussion today, what kinds of situations call for a deliverance from God? When do we need to cry out to the God of deliverances?

2. What did you learn from the example of Nehemiah?

3. What is the background of Psalm 34?

4. What was your favorite verse in Psalm 34?

5. What kinds of fears do you deal with and how does Psalm 34:4 offer encouragement?

6. Did you have a favorite insight from the devotional reading?

DAY 2: Those Who Cry Out

1. Have someone in the group read Psalm 34:6. What did you learn about the word "poor" in the Hebrew?

2. Share what you learned from the verses about crying out to the Lord.

3. Have you ever had a time when the Lord has saved you out of a trouble as a result of crying out to Him?

DAY 3: Those Who Taste and See

1. Have someone read Psalm 34:8.

2. What does it mean to taste and see that the Lord is good? You had the opportunity to read some powerful verses—what did you learn?

3. What was your favorite insight from Day 3?

DAY 4: Those Who Seek the Lord

1. Have someone in your group read Psalm 34:10.

2. What did you learn about the Lord from the verses you looked at in Day 4?

3. What does it mean to "seek the Lord"?

4. What was your favorite insight from the devotional reading in Day 4?

5. What kind of hope does this promise in Psalm 34:10 offer?

DAY 5: Those Who Are Righteous

1. Have someone read Psalm 34:17.

2. What is your favorite phrase in the hymn, Amazing Grace, and why?

3. What does it mean to be righteous?

4. Describe what Christ has done for us.

5. What was your favorite privilege that you discovered in Psalm 34?

6. What is the most important truth you learned in Day 5?

DAYS 6 AND 7: Devotional Reading by John Henry Jowett

1. What was your favorite verse, insight, or quote from your quiet times this week?

2. What did you learn from the excerpt by John Henry Jowett?

3. Close your time together in prayer.

Week Six: Hope When You are in Darkness

The goal for your discussion is to help your group understand the powerful truths in Psalm 91 that will give them hope when they are in darkness and experience what some have called the dark night of the soul.

DAY 1: You Dwell in the Shelter of the Most High

1. Open your discussion with prayer. Share briefly about your discussion last week about how to have hope when you need deliverance. We saw that David, who was the author of Psalm 34, knew what it was to need deliverance as he was chased by King Saul. David learned that God is the God of deliverances. Now, this week, we have spent time in Psalm 91, a psalm that will give you hope when you are in darkness. Have someone in your group read Psalm 91:1. Definitions for some of the words in this verse were included in your quiet time. What was your favorite insight from the meanings of these words?

2. What did you learn about your shelter, your hiding place in the Lord, from the verses you looked at on Day 1?

3. Why is it that "calm in the midst of a storm" is such a good picture of the true meaning of peace?

4. What helps you understand what peace really is? Why is there peace in the Lord?

5. In what ways do you need the shelter of the Lord right now in your life?

DAY 2: You Abide in the Shadow of the Almighty

1. What does it mean to "abide" in the shadow of the Almighty?

2. What did you learn about the Lord in Psalm 91 that gives you hope in the darkness of life?

3. What did you learn from the words of Spurgeon and Jowett?

DAY 3: You Trust in Your Refuge and Fortress

1. Have someone in your group read Psalm 91:2.

2. The great truth is that even in the times of darkness, the Lord is your refuge and fortress. What was your favorite phrase in Amy Carmichael's words?

3. What did you learn about the Lord in the verses on Day Three and how will these truths help you to trust the Lord more?

4. Where in your own life do you find it most difficult to trust the Lord and what have you learned that will help you to trust the Lord more?

DAY 4: You Hide Under His Wings

1. Have someone in your group read Psalm 91:4.

2. You had the opportunity to meditate on the words of the hymn, Be Still My Soul. What was your favorite phrase in this hymn this week?

3. What does the Lord's care and protection of you mean to you today? Where in your own life do you need His own care and protection the most?

4. What was your favorite quote in Day 4?

DAY 5: You Rest in a Secure Place on High

1. Have someone in your group read Psalm 91:14.

2. What truths did you learn from the devotional reading and the verses in today's quiet time that can give you hope in the midst of a difficult trial?

DAYS 6 AND 7: Devotional Reading by Kenneth Wuest

1. What was your favorite verse, insight, or quote from your quiet times this week?

2. What did you learn from the excerpt by Kenneth Wuest?

3. What is the most important truth you learned from Psalm 91 this week? How can you apply it in your own life?

4. Close in prayer.

Week Seven: Hope When You Need Help

The goal for your discussion is to help your group understand the powerful truths in Psalm 121 that will give them hope when they need help.

DAY 1: Lift Up Your Eyes

1. Open your discussion with prayer. Share briefly about all that we have been looking at in the psalms to have a heart that hopes in God. Begin with the definition of hope: holding on with patient expectation. Ask your group to share some of the things that they have learned about hope. Then, share briefly as a summary how we learned from Psalm 139 that the Lord knows us, He is with us, He created us, He has a plan for us, and He thinks about us. And then, we learned in Psalm 31 that we can have hope when we are in trouble because of the eternal perspective found in the promises of God. We learned from David in Psalm 18 that the Lord will rescue us when we are discouraged. Psalm 34 gave us the hope that God is the God of deliverances. He saves us out of fear and troubles as we seek Him. When we are in darkness, we learned from Psalm 91 that the Lord is our shelter and our hiding place.

2. Now, this week, we have spent time in Psalm 121, a psalm that will give you hope when you need help. Have someone in your group read Psalm 121.

3. Ask your group what they learned from the example of Corrie ten Boom.

4. Why does where we look make such a difference in a trial?

5. Where are we to look according to the verses we looked at this week?

6. What helps you to lift up your eyes to the Lord in the midst of a trial?

DAY 2: You Have a Helper

1. Have someone in your group read Psalm 121:2. In Day 2, we looked at the truth that the Lord is our helper.

2. What was your favorite phrase in the prayer under *Prepare Your Heart*?

3. In what ways is the Lord a help according to Psalm 121?

4. What did you learn about the Lord's help in your life from the other verses you studied?

DAY 3: He is Your Keeper

1. In Day 3 you looked at the Lord as your keeper. What does it mean that the Lord "keeps" you?

2. What are ways He keeps us according to the verses you looked at in Day 3?

3. What was your favorite quote from your quiet time in Day 3?

DAY 4: The Lord is Your Shade

1. Have someone in your group read Psalm 121:5. What meant the most to you in thinking about the Lord as your "shade?"

2. What kind of shade does the Lord provide for us?

3. Why do we need the shade of the Lord?

4. What meant the most to you from the story about the china?

DAY 5: All the Way to Forever

1. What did it mean to you to know that "the Lord will guard your going out and your coming in from this time forth and forever?" How does that truth bring you comfort in your life right now?

2. What encouraged you from Psalm 37:23-25 and what was your favorite phrase from the different translations?

3. How does knowing the Lord is with you *all the way to forever* give you hope?

DAYS 6 AND 7: Devotional Reading by Horatius Bonar

1. What was your favorite verse, insight, or quote from your quiet times this week?

2. What was your favorite insight from the words of Charles Haddon Spurgeon?

3. Share one time in your life where the Lord has been your help.

4. What is the greatest area of your life where you need the help of the Lord?

5. Close your time together in prayer.

Week Eight: Hope for All Your Needs

The goal of your discussion is to help your group understand that there is always hope no matter what they need. The focus of your discussion will be the powerful promises in Psalm 23. You will want to allow time for sharing all that those in your group have learned in *A Heart That Hopes in God.*

DAY 1: When There is No One

1. Open your discussion with prayer. Begin by expressing how much you've enjoyed leading the group and sharing together during this journey through the Psalms. And share how wonderful the discussions have been. As you discuss together for one last time in A Heart That Hopes In God, ask your group what has been their favorite part of this study.

2. This week we spent time in Psalm 23, a favorite psalm for many. Have someone in the group read Psalm 23.

3. Why do you think this psalm has been a favorite for so many?

4. What did you learn about the Lord in Psalm 23?

5. What did you learn about Jesus in John 10?

6. Why do you need a shepherd?

7. What was your favorite quote from your quiet time in Day 1?

DAY 2: When You are Tired and Worn Out

1. What did you learn about rest from Psalm 23:2-3?

2. What did you learn about rest in the verses from Matthew and Mark?

3. What was your favorite quote from the devotional reading?

DAY 3: When You Face the Shadow of Death

1. What encouragement do we have from Psalm 23 if we are in the valley of the shadow of death?

2. What is the value of the rod and the staff?

3. What did you learn about the care of the Lord from the verses you read in the Bible in your Day 3 quiet time?

4. What was your favorite truth in Day 3 that brings encouragement to you?

DAY 4: When Your Enemy Comes Against You

1. Have someone read Psalm 23:5 out loud to the class. You had the opportunity to look at different translations of this verse—what was your favorite phrase in the translations?

2. What was your favorite insight related to the table that the Lord prepares in the presence of your enemies?

3. What did you learn about spiritual warfare in Ephesians 6:10-18?

4. What helps you the most when it seems as though everything is against you?

5. Why do you think prayer is important in spiritual warfare?

6. What was your favorite quote from Day 4?

DAY 5: Hope's Bright Conclusion

1. According to Psalm 23:6, what is the hope that you can hold on to no matter what happens in your life? Why is it called "hope's bright conclusion?"

2. What did you learn about heaven and eternal life from the verses in John and Revelation?

3. What was your favorite quote from your Day 5 quiet time?

DAYS 6 AND 7: Devotional Reading by John Henry Jowett

1. What encouraged your from the excerpt from John Henry Jowett?

2. You had an opportunity to take some time and leaf through these eights weeks of quiet times to look at all you have learned. What have we learned about hope in this study?

3. What is the most important truth you have learned about hope in this book of quiet times? What will you take with you? (If you have a visual aid such as a whiteboard, you might even write these truths out for your class to see).

4. How did God answer the prayer that you wrote in your letter to Him at the beginning of the study?

5. What will you take with you from *A Heart That Hopes In God*? What will you always remember?

6. Close in prayer.

RECOMMENDED BOOKS ON PSALMS

I love the Psalms and have collected many books and commentaries on the Psalms over the years. I use them often in my quiet time as added encouragement and study in drawing near to the Lord. Here are some of my favorites. I encourage you to make the Psalms a permanent part of your quiet time.

A Psalm In Your Heart by George O. Wood (Springfield, MO: Gospel Publishing House 2008)

A Shepherd Looks at Psalm 23 by Phillip Keller (Grand Rapids, MI: Zondervan Publishing House 1970)

Answering God: The Psalms as a Tool for Prayer by Eugene Peterson (San Francisco: Harper & Row 1989)

Choice Notes on the Psalms by F.B. Meyer (Grand Rapids, MI: Kregel Publications 1984)

Commentary on the Psalms by Allan Harman (Scotland, Great Britain: Christian Focus Publications Ltd. 1998)

Commentary on Psalms by Joseph A. Alexander (Grand Rapids, MI: Kregel Publications 1991)

Commentary on the Psalms by J.J. Stewart Perowne (Grand Rapids, MI: Kregel Publications 1989)

Daily Prayer and Praise, Volumes 1 and 2 by Henry Law (Carlisle, PA: The Banner of Truth Trust 2000)

How to Read the Psalms by Tremper Longman III (Downers Grove, IL: InterVarsity Press 1988)

Notes on the Psalms by G. Campbell Morgan (Tarrytown, NY: Fleming H. Revell Company)

Psalms: A Devotional Commentary by Herbert Lockyer (Grand Rapids, MI: Kregel Publications 1993)

Psalms—A Handbook on the Book of Psalms by Robert G. Bratcher and William D. Reyburn (New York, NY: United Bible Societies 1991)

Psalms: The Prayer Book of the Bible by Dietrich Bonhoeffer (Minneapolis, MN: Augsburg Publishing House 1970)

Psalms: Volumes 1 and 2 by Derek Kidner (Downers Grove, IL: InterVarsity Press 1973)

Psalms, Volumes 1 and 2 by James Montgomery Boice (Grand Rapids, MI: Baker Book House 1994)

Reflections on the Psalms by C.S. Lewis (New York: Harcourt, Brace & Company 1958)

The Shepherd Psalm by F.B. Meyer (New Canaan, CT: Keats Publishing 1979)

The Treasury of David by Charles Haddon Spurgeon

NOTES

WEEK 1

1. Steve Miller, *C.H. Spurgeon on Spiritual Leadership* (Chicago: Moody Press, 2003), pp. 74-75.
2. Charles Haddon Spurgeon, *Beside Still Waters: Words of Comfort for the Soul* (Nashville: Thomas Nelson Publishers 2000), May 18.
3. Charles Haddon Spurgeon, *Beside Still Waters: Words of Comfort for the Soul*, May 17.
4. Spiros Zodhiates, *The Hebrew-Greek Key Study Bible* (Chattanooga: AMG Publishers, 1984, 1990) p. 1831.
5. John Henry Jowett, *The Silver Lining*, (New York: Fleming H. Revell, 1907) pp. 133-134.
6. Isaac Watts, *The Psalms and Hymns of Isaac Watts* (Morgan: Soli Deo Gloria Publications, 1997) pp. 218-219.
7. Mrs. Charles Cowman, *Streams in the Desert* (The Oriental Missionary Society) p. 27.
8. Mrs. Charles Cowman, *Streams in the Desert*, p. 93.
9. F.B. Meyer, *Daily Prayers* (Wheaton: Harold Shaw Publishers, 1995) p. 18.
10. Charles Haddon Spurgeon, *Beside Still Waters: Words of Comfort for the Soul*, June 4.
11. Charles Haddon Spurgeon, *Beside Still Waters: Words of Comfort for the Soul*, March 21.

WEEK 2

1. F.B. Meyer, *Choice Notes on the Psalms* (Grand Rapids: Kregel Publications, 1984), pp. 167-168.
2. Arthur Bennett ed., *The Valley of Vision* (Carlisle: The Banner of Truth Trust, 1975), Used by permission.
3. A.W. Tozer, *The Pursuit of God* (Camp Hill: Christian Publications, 1993) pp. 62-66.
4. Amy Carmichael, *Ponnamal* (London: Morgan & Scott Ltd., n.d.) p. 9.
5. Henry Law, *Daily Prayer and Praise Volume 2* (Carlisle: The Banner of Truth Trust, 2000) p. 259.
6. Amy Carmichael, *Ponnamal*, p. vii.
7. Henry Law, *Daily Prayer and Praise Volume 2*, pp. 259-260.
8. Amy Carmichael, *Gold by Moonlight* (Fort Washington: Christian Literature Crusade, n.d.), p. 75. Used by permission.
9. Nancy Speigelberg, *Fanfare: A Celebration of Belief* (Portland: Multnomah Press, 1981).

WEEK 3

1. Annie Johnson Flint, *Best-Loved Poems*, (Toronto: Evangelical Publishers) p. 13.
2. Vreni Schiess, *Songs in the Night*, (Palm Desert: Person to Person Books, 1985) June 2.
3. Vreni Schiess, *Songs in the Night*, June 2.
4. See *A Heart To See Forever* by Catherine Martin (Palm Desert: Quiet Time Ministries, 2003).
5. Octavius Winslow, *Help Heavenward* (Carlisle: The Banner of Truth Trust, 2000), pp. 1, 10.
6. See *Six Secrets to a Powerful Quiet Time* by Catherine Martin to learn all about how to really have a quiet time. (Eugene: Harvest House Publishers, 2005).
7. Catherine Marshall ed., *The Prayers of Peter Marshall*, (Grand Rapids: Chosen Books, 1982), p. 40.
8. F.B. Meyer, *Choice Notes on the Psalms*, (Grand Rapids: Kregel Publications, 1984) p. 43.
9. Spiros Zodhiates, *The Hebrew-Greek Key Study Bible* (Chattanooga: AMG Publishers, 1984, 1990) p. 1765.

10. Annie Johnson Flint, *Best-Loved Poems*, (Toronto: Evangelical Publishers) pp. 18-19.

11. Octavius Winslow, *Help Heavenward*, p. 71.

12. Octavius Winslow, *Help Heavenward*, pp. 66-67, 70-71.

WEEK 4

1. Jill Morgan, *A Man of the Word* (New York: Fleming H. Revell Company, 1951) pp. 39-40.

2. F.B. Meyer, *Daily Prayers* (Wheaton: Harold Shaw Publishers, 1995) p. 83.

3. Mrs. Charles Cowman, *Streams in the Desert* (The Oriental Missionary Society) March 22.

4. Oswald Chambers, *Christian Disciplines* (Grand Rapids: Discovery House Publishers, 1995) p. 115.

5. Oswald Chambers, *Christian Disciplines,* pp. 117-118.

6. Mrs. Charles Cowman, *Streams in the Desert*, January 24.

7. Mrs. Charles Cowman, *Streams in the Desert*, June 6.

8. Catherine Marshall ed., *The Prayers of Peter Marshall*, (Grand Rapids: Chosen Books, 1982), p. 11.

9. Charles Haddon Spurgeon, *Beside Still Waters: Words of Comfort for the Soul* (Nashville: Thomas Nelson Publishers 2000) November 18.

10. A.W. Tozer, *The Pursuit of God* (Camp Hill: Christian Publications, 1993) pp. 50-51.

11. Charles Spurgeon, *Beside Still Waters: Words of Comfort for the Soul*, June 26.

12. Charles Spurgeon, *The Treasury of David Volume 1* (McLean: MacDonald Publishing Company, n.d.) pp. 244-246.

13. James Montgomery Boice, *Psalms, Volume 1 (Psalms 1-41)* (Grand Rapids, MI: Baker Book House, 1994) pp. 158-159.

WEEK 5

1. James Montgomery Boice, *Psalms, Volumes 1 (Psalms 1-41)* (Grand Rapids, MI: Baker Book House, 1994), p. 295.

2. Charles Haddon Spurgeon, *Beside Still Waters: Words of Comfort for the Soul* (Nashville: Thomas Nelson Publishers 2000), March 14.

3. AMG Bible Illustrations: Bible Illustrations Series (Chattanooga: AMG Publishers 2000 Electronic edition Logos Library System).

4. James Montgomery Boice, *Psalms, Volume 1 (Psalms 1-41)* (Grand Rapids, MI: Baker Book House, 1994) p. 294.

5. E.M. Bounds, *The Possibilities of Prayer* (New York: Fleming H. Revell Company, 1923) p. 15.

6. Mrs. Charles Cowman, *Streams in the Desert* (The Oriental Missionary Society) July 27.

7. Spiros Zodhiates, *The Hebrew-Greek Key Study Bible* (Chattanooga: AMG Publishers, 1984, 1990) p. 1729.

8. Spiros Zodhiates, *The Hebrew-Greek Key Study Bible*, p. 1853.

9. James Montgomery Boice, *Psalms, Volume 1 (Psalms 1-41)*, p. 297.

10. Annie Johnson Flint, *Best-Loved Poems*, (Toronto: Evangelical Publishers) p. 31.

11. Alan Redpath, *The Making of a Man of God*, (Old Tappan: Fleming H. Revell Company, 1962) p. 93.

12. Charles Spurgeon, *The Treasury of David* (McLean: MacDonald Publishing Company, n.d.) pp. 124-125.

13. F.B. Meyer, *Daily Prayers* (Wheaton: Harold Shaw Publishers, 1995) p. 126.

14. Miles J. Stanford, *The Complete Works of Miles J. Stanford*, (Galaxie Software, 2002).

15. John Henry Jowett, *Life in the Heights—Studies in the Epistles* (New York: George H. Doran Company, 1925), pp. 197-202.

WEEK 6

1. Herbert Lockyer, *Psalms: A Devotional Commentary* (Grand Rapids: Kregel Publications, 1993), p. 315.

2. Charles Spurgeon, *The Treasury of David*, (McLean: MacDonald Publishing Company, n.d.) Psalm 91.

3. F.B. Meyer, *Daily Prayers* (Wheaton: Harold Shaw Publishers, 1995) p. 60.

4. Berit Kjos, *A Wardrobe from the King* (Wheaton: Victor Books, 1988), pp. 45-46.

5. Charles Haddon Spurgeon, *Behold The Throne of Grace—Spurgeon's Prayers and Hymns* (London and Edinburgh: Marshall, Morgan & Scott Ltd. n.d.) pp. 59-60.

6. John Henry Jowett, *Life in the Heights* (New York: George H. Doran Company, 1925) pp. 99-101.

7. Amy Carmichael, *Mountain Breezes: The Collected Poems of Amy Carmichael* (Fort Washington: Christian Literature Crusade, 1999) p. 25. Used by permission.

8. A.W. Tozer, *The Pursuit of God* (Camp Hill: Christian Publications, 1993) pp. 52, 58-59.

9. Charles Haddon Spurgeon, *Beside Still Waters: Words of Comfort for the Soul* (Nashville: Thomas Nelson Publishers 2000), March 23.

10. Miles J. Stanford, *The Complete Works of Miles J. Stanford*, (Galaxie Software, 2002).

11. Kenneth S. Wuest, *Wuest's Word Studies from the Greek New Testament*, Volume 3 (Grand Rapids: Eerdmans Publishing Company, 1977) pp. 103-104.

WEEK 7

1. Charles Spurgeon, *The Treasury of David Volume 3* (McLean: MacDonald Publishing Company, n.d.) p. 353.

2. Arthur Bennett ed., *The Valley of Vision* (Carlisle: The Banner of Truth Trust, 1975) page 101. Used by permission.

3. F.B. Meyer, *Choice Notes on the Psalms*, (Grand Rapids: Kregel Publications, 1984) p. 147.

4. J.J. Stewart Perowne, *Commentary on the Psalms* (Grand Rapids: Kregel Publications, 1989), p. 373.

5. F.B. Meyer, *Choice Notes on the Psalms*, p. 147.

6. Mrs. Charles Cowman, *Springs in the Valley*, (Oriental Missionary Society) November 12.

7. Herbert Lockyer, *Psalms: A Devotional Commentary* (Grand Rapids: Kregel Publications, 1993), p. 626.

8. F.B. Meyer, *Daily Prayers* (Wheaton: Harold Shaw Publishers, 1995) p. 56.

9. Charles Spurgeon, *The Treasury of David Volume 3*, p. 354.

10. Mrs. Charles Cowman, *Springs in the Valley*, (Oriental Missionary Society) July 4.

WEEK 8

1. F.B. Meyer, *Choice Notes on the Psalms*, (Grand Rapids: Kregel Publications, 1984) pp. 33-34.

2. Charles Spurgeon, *The Treasury of David Volume 1* (McLean: MacDonald Publishing Company, n.d.) p. 353.

3. Henry Law, *Daily Prayer and Praise Volume 1* (Carlisle: The Banner of Truth Trust, 2000) p. 115.

4. Henry Law, *Daily Prayer and Praise Volume 1*, pp. 116-117.

5. Charles Spurgeon, *The Treasury of David Volume 1*, p. 354.

6. F.B. Meyer, *Daily Prayers* (Wheaton: Harold Shaw Publishers, 1995) p. 115.

7. Henry Law, *Daily Prayer and Praise Volume 1* (Carlisle: The Banner of Truth Trust, 2000) p. 117.

8. F.B. Meyer, *Choice Notes on the Psalms*, (Grand Rapids: Kregel Publications, 1984) p. 34.

9. Henry Law, *Daily Prayer and Praise Volume 1*, pp. 117-118.

10. Charles Spurgeon, *The Treasury of David, Volume 1,* pp. 356-357.

11. Catherine Martin, *Six Secrets to a Powerful Quiet Time* (Eugene: Harvest House Publishers, 2005). Quiet Time Ministries resource information at www.quiettime.org.

12. More information about quiet time studies by Catherine Martin at Quiet Time Ministries www.quiettime.org. (Books of quiet times include *A Heart that Hopes in God, Run Before the Wind, Trusting in the Names of God, Passionate Prayer, Pilgrimage of the Heart, Revive My Heart, A Heart that Dances, A Heart on Fire,* and *A Heart to See Forever.*

13. John Henry Jowett, *The Silver Lining,* (New York: Fleming H. Revell, 1907) pp. 134-135.

❧ ACKNOWLEDGMENTS ❧

How does a book like *A Heart That Hopes In God* come about? It takes years of God etching these principles from the Word of God on the heart in such a way that it is lived out in life. I have long desired to begin a new series of quiet times for the busy person to use in their quiet time to go deep with God and grow in their intimate relationship with Him. The result is this new series of quiet times: A Quiet Time Experience. The first in the series is *A Heart That Hopes In God*.

Thank you to my precious family; David, Mother, Dad, Rob, Kayla, Christopher, Eloise, Ann, Andy, Keegan, and James. Thank you especially for your unconditional love and encouragement as I write books and share the message that God has laid on my heart in my quiet times alone with Him.

I want to especially thank my husband, David, for your love, wisdom, and brilliance as together we run this race set before us. And thank you for the beautiful cover design of *A Heart That Hopes In God*.

I am so very thankful to our Quiet Time Ministries staff team for serving the Lord together with me, especially in these days when so many incredible opportunities are opening up for this ministry. Thank you Kayla Branscum, Paula Zillmer, Shirley Peters, Conni Hudson, Cindy Clark, Sandy Fallon, Karen Darras, and Kelly Abeyratne. Kayla, thank you for coming alongside me many years ago in Quiet Time Ministries as my assistant. You have a thousand gifts and talents that you use to the glory of God. I am so thankful to Him for you.

A special thanks to Charlie Branscum who has tirelessly served the Lord in so many ways with Quiet Time Ministries. And Cindy, thank you for your unparalleled vision for what God can do in and through us as we run our race. Shirley, thank you for praying years ago, when Quiet Time Ministries was just an idea from the Lord, that it would become a ministry that God would use to reach the world. Kelly, thank you for your faithful prayers for me and for Quiet Time Ministries. And Conni, thank you for encouraging me to finish writing that first book of quiet times, *Pilgrimage of the Heart*, so many years ago. I sure am glad I listened to you.

And then, thank you for my dear friends who have offered such words of truth, encouragement, and hope that I have needed all along the way: Beverly Trupp, Andy Kotner, Dottie McDowell, and Vonette Bright.

Thank you to those of you have shared in the journey of Quiet Time Ministries: John and Betty Mann, Stefanie Kelly, Sandi Rogers, Myra Murphy, and Kathleen Otremba.

Thank you to the Board of Directors of Quiet Time Ministries: David Martin, Conni Hudson, Shirley Peters, and Jane Lyons, for your faithfulness in this ministry. And thank you to all who have partnered with me both financially and prayerfully in Quiet Time Ministries. You have helped make possible this idea the Lord gave me so many years ago called Quiet Time Ministries. Thank you to the Enriching Your Quiet Time magazine staff for helping develop these ideas on hope: Shirley Peters, Conni Hudson, Maurine Cromwell, and Cay Hough.

Thank you Shirley Peters for leading our pilot study of *A Heart That Hopes In God*. I learned so much from your questions and leading of us in these truths in the Psalms. Thank you to those who piloted this quiet time experience: Kelly Abeyratne, Jodi Adams, Shirley Baker, Kayla Branscum, Melissa Brown, Ceil Burns, Cindy Clark, Donna Delahanty, Jean Gunderson, Joan Hill, Sandra Hill, Conni Hudson, Dawn Ivie, Davida Kreisler, Sally Leachman, Kay McCann, Yvonne Richards, Sherylen Yoak, Paula Zillmer, Francene Fisher, Julie Airis, Georgeann DeWoody, Sharon Hastings, Betty Mann, Myra Murphy, Bev Trupp, Cay Hough, Loretta Harrell, Connie Sparks, Nancy Brown, Cheryl Clark, and Dave Petrie.

Thank you to the staff at Southwest Community Church for loving the Lord. Thank you to the women at Southwest Community Church—it is such a joy and privilege to serve the Lord together with you.

And then, thank you to those who have been such a huge help to me in the writing and publishing of books: Jim Smoke whose advice and help have, by God's grace, completely altered the course of my life and Greg Johnson, my agent, who has come alongside me and Quiet Time Ministries to help in the goals that the Lord has laid on my heart.

A special thanks to all those leaders who answer God's call to lead others and challenge them to draw near to God, study His Word, and live for His glory.

Finally, thank you to all those saints who have the run the race before and shown me that I could stand strong and hope in God and His Word; especially Corrie ten Boom, Darlene Deibler Rose, Horatio Spafford, Charles Haddon Spurgeon, John Henry Jowett, Octavius Winslow, Amy Carmichael, and Annie Johnson Flint. May your tribe increase.

JOURNAL

"Pour out your heart like water in the presence of the Lord" — Lamentations 2:19 NIV

JOURNAL

"Pour out your heart like water in the presence of the Lord" — Lamentations 2:19 NIV

JOURNAL

"Pour out your heart like water in the
presence of the Lord" — Lamentations 2:19 NIV

JOURNAL

"Pour out your heart like water in the
presence of the Lord" — Lamentations 2:19 NIV

JOURNAL

"Pour out your heart like water in the
presence of the Lord" — Lamentations 2:19 NIV

SIX SECRETS TO A POWERFUL QUIET TIME ©2005

JOURNAL

"Pour out your heart like water in the
presence of the Lord" — Lamentations 2:19 NIV

....

....

....

....

....

....

....

....

....

....

....

....

....

....

....

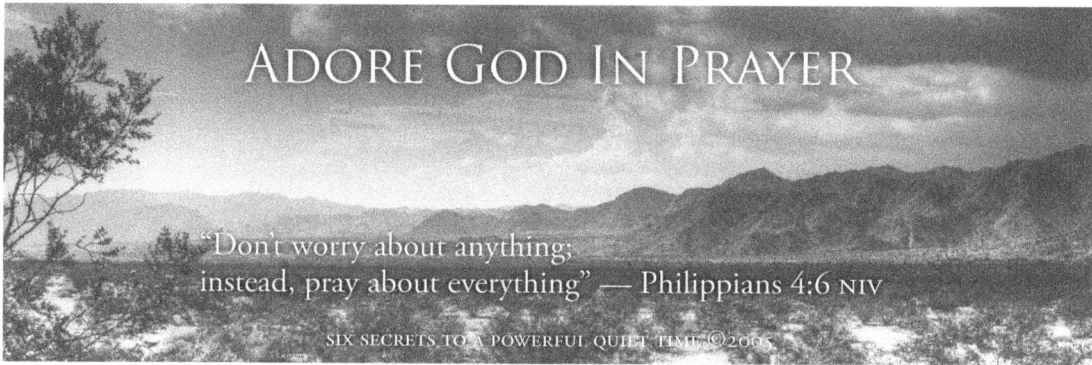

ADORE GOD IN PRAYER

"Don't worry about anything;
instead, pray about everything" — Philippians 4:6 NIV

SIX SECRETS TO A POWERFUL QUIET TIME ©2005

Prayer for _____

Date: Topic:
Scripture:
Request:

Answer:

_____

Date: Topic:
Scripture:
Request:

Answer:

_____

Date: Topic:
Scripture:
Request:

Answer:

_____

Date: Topic:
Scripture:
Request:

Answer:

_____

Date: Topic:
Scripture:
Request:

Answer:

_____

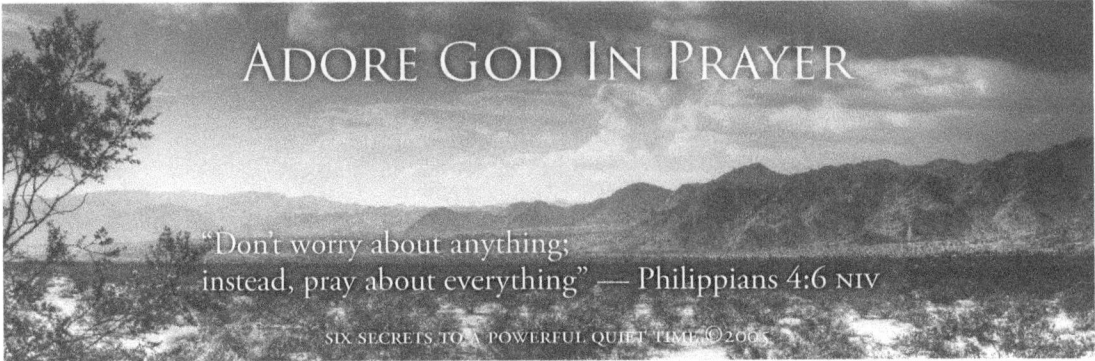

*Prayer for*_____

Date: Topic:
Scripture:
Request:

Answer:
_____

Date: Topic:
Scripture:
Request:

Answer:
_____

Date: Topic:
Scripture:
Request:

Answer:
_____

Date: Topic:
Scripture:
Request:

Answer:
_____

Date: Topic:
Scripture:
Request:

Answer:
_____

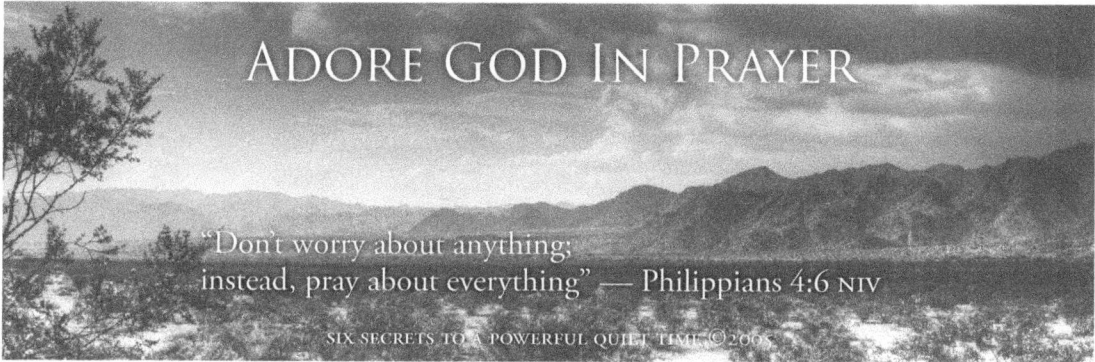

ADORE GOD IN PRAYER

"Don't worry about anything;
instead, pray about everything" — Philippians 4:6 NIV

*Prayer for*_____

Date: Topic:
Scripture:
Request:

Answer:

Date: Topic:
Scripture:
Request:

Answer:

Date: Topic:
Scripture:
Request:

Answer:

Date: Topic:
Scripture:
Request:

Answer:

Date: Topic:
Scripture:
Request:

Answer:

ADORE GOD IN PRAYER

"Don't worry about anything;
instead, pray about everything" — Philippians 4:6 NIV

SIX SECRETS TO A POWERFUL QUIET TIME ©2005

*Prayer for*_____

Date: Topic:
Scripture:
Request:

Answer:

Date: Topic:
Scripture:
Request:

Answer:

Date: Topic:
Scripture:
Request:

Answer:

Date: Topic:
Scripture:
Request:

Answer:

Date: Topic:
Scripture:
Request:

Answer:

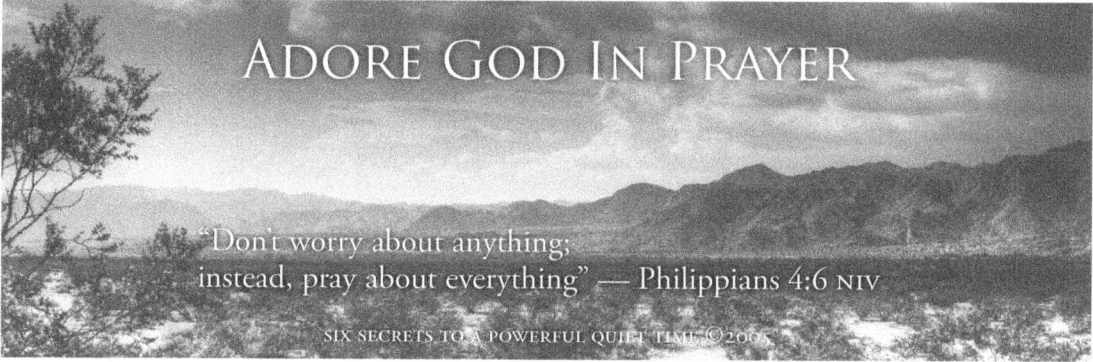

*Prayer for*_____

Date: Topic:
Scripture:
Request:

Answer:

_____

Date: Topic:
Scripture:
Request:

Answer:

_____

Date: Topic:
Scripture:
Request:

Answer:

_____

Date: Topic:
Scripture:
Request:

Answer:

_____

Date: Topic:
Scripture:
Request:

Answer:

_____

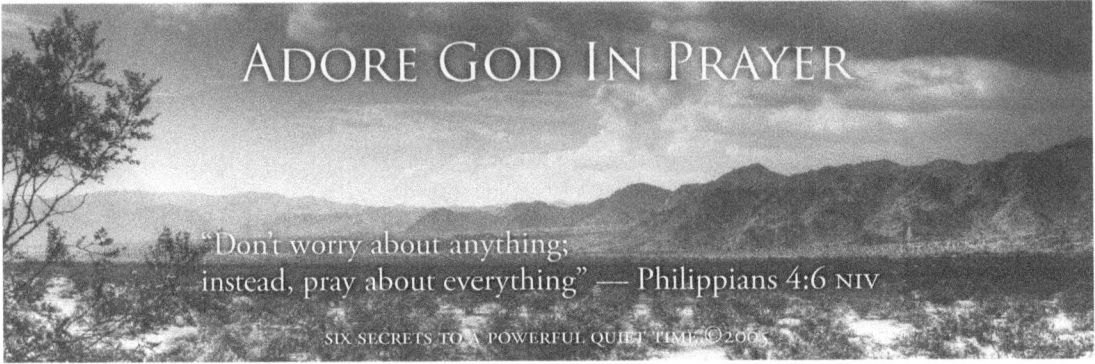

ADORE GOD IN PRAYER

"Don't worry about anything;
instead, pray about everything" — Philippians 4:6 NIV

Prayer for_____

Date: Topic:
Scripture:
Request:

Answer:

_____

Date: Topic:
Scripture:
Request:

Answer:

_____

Date: Topic:
Scripture:
Request:

Answer:

_____

Date: Topic:
Scripture:
Request:

Answer:

_____

Date: Topic:
Scripture:
Request:

Answer:

_____

www.ingramcontent.com/pod-product-compliance
Lightning Source LLC
Chambersburg PA
CBHW062038090426
42740CB00016B/2942